THE HORSE OWNER'S
PROBLEM SOLVER

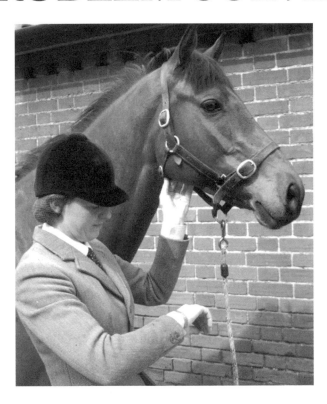

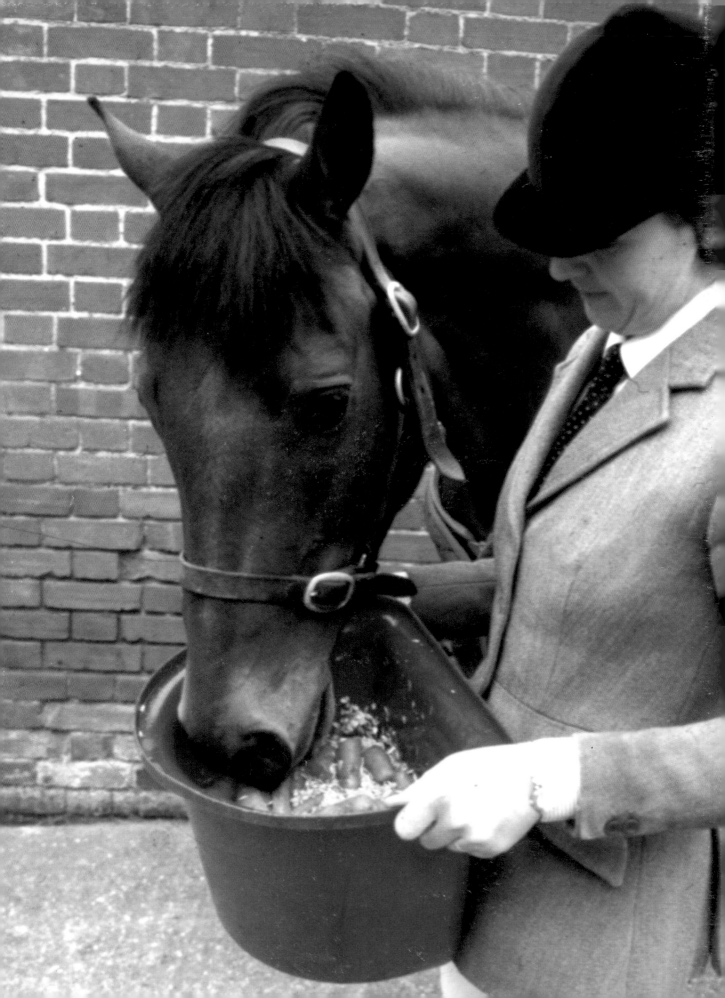

THE HORSE OWNER'S
PROBLEM SOLVER

Provides practical solutions to the most common
problems relating to horse care and management

VANESSA BRITTON

DAVID & CHARLES

CONTENTS

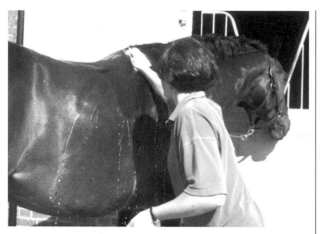

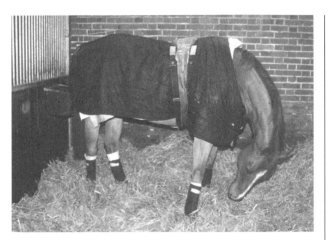

PART 3 Health and Veterinary Care   82

PART 4 Feeding and Nutrition   128

All illustrations by Vanessa Britton except:
p29(right) Champion Tails; pp 6–7, 29(left &
centre), 68, 74–5, 128–9, 137 Kit Houghton;
pp 93(all), 101, 109, 110, 111,112 Tony Pavord;
p95 Derek Croucher

A DAVID & CHARLES BOOK

First published in the UK in 1998

A catalogue record for this book is
available from the British Library

ISBN 0 7153 0614 6

Design by Visual Image
Printed in Spain by Graficas Reunidas S.A.
for David & Charles
Brunel House Newton Abbot Devon

STABLE

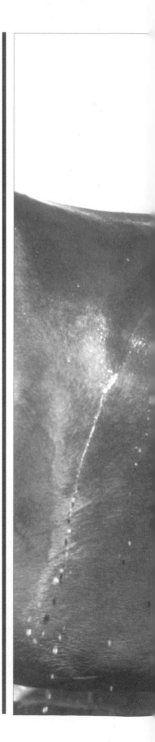

Horse Behaviour
Head-shy
A clean pair of heels
Stroppy at shows
Nasty nipping

Stabling
Planting the feet
Vice prevention
Windsucking
Door knocker!
Pulling back
Basic stable safety
Dust allergies

Grooming
Waving goodbye to winter
  woollies
Sensitive skin
The benefits of banging
Improving the coat
Careful cleaning

Bathing
Washing worries

Plaiting
Baggy plaits

Manes and Tails
Pulling problems
No tail

Clipping & Trimming
Clipper-phobic
Whipping off whiskers
Excessive sweating

Bitting
Faulty fitting
Pinching the corners
Rollered mouthpieces
Sticking out the tongue
Double jointed
Tongue over the bit

Saddle Fitting
A perfect fit

Rugging
Ripping yarns
Storing rugs

Travelling
Confidence crisis
In a sweat
Horsebox horrors

Insurance
Spoilt for choice
Excessive excess
Immediate cover
Tack theft
Types of treatment
Vets' views

Part 1:
MANAGEMENT

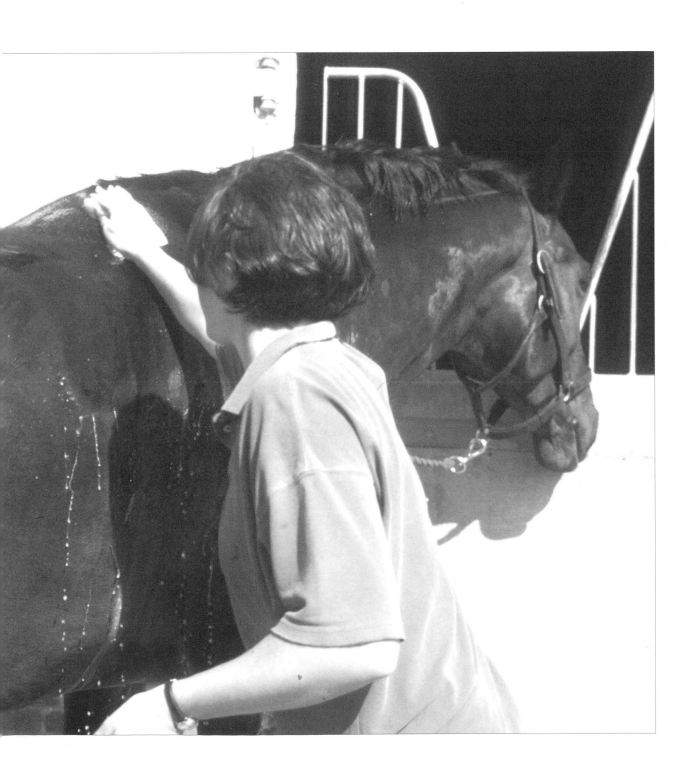

Head-shy

PROBLEM   Some horses are extremely head-shy and cannot bear to be touched around the face or ears. How should this problem be tackled?

Horses that cannot bear to be touched around the head or ears often try to put their heads right up in the air out of reach when the bridle is being fitted

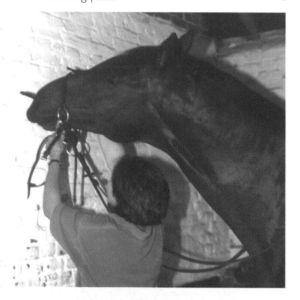

SOLUTION   The first thing to do is to establish a cause, which is usually one of three:

■ the horse has a physical problem;
■ the horse may have been slapped round the face by a previous, uncaring owner;
■ the horse may have banged his head in the stable, field or box and become nervous.

Head-shy problems may also be caused because the horse has been badly broken in – he has been roughly or ineptly handled at the outset of his training experience, and so has been taught to be *nervous*. Alternatively his bridle may be ill-fitting and uncomfortable; a grakle or a flash noseband fitted too tightly will often make a horse head-shy.

A physical problem should be discounted before other causes are investigated. This is a case for the veterinary surgeon who will be looking for things such as ear-mites; ear infection; tooth problems; deficient eyesight; conjunctivitis; sinusitis; and parasitic skin conditions. Once the horse has been treated, he should be happy to allow you to handle his head again, although he may be a little cautious at first, so great tact and gentle handling are needed.

Where a horse has been slapped or otherwise ill-treated, only careful, patient and kind handling over a long period of time will see any improvement. The horse's trust and confidence will need to be restored before he learns to accept routine tasks such as bridling and grooming the head. Putting on the bridle is probably the most difficult task with a head-shy horse, and obviously remedying the situation is going to take a long time, so a way of fitting the bridle must be found. To start with the headcollar should be left on and the owner should talk to the horse soothingly all the time. The bridle should be supple, and the reins and bit removed thus avoiding too many pieces having

TIP

If none of these methods work then a simple bridle of just a headpiece with bit clips (not hook studs) and a bit may have to be used to start with. The headpiece is put over the middle of the horse's neck and the owner's left hand restrains the nose. The headpiece is then moved forwards and the browband placed over the ears. The bit (preferably a rubber or soft nathe one coated in molasses or treacle if necessary) is then clipped onto the off-side, encouraged into the mouth and quickly clipped onto the left cheekpiece.

to be put over the horse's head. A straw bale to stand on may be required, although the owner should be careful not to jump up onto the bale and startle the horse.

The right hand should be placed under the horse's neck, taking hold of both the cheekpieces, while an assistant holds the horse with a leadrope from the headcollar. Gradually the headpiece can be drawn up the face and gently eased over one ear and then the other. As there is no pull from the bit, the headpiece and browband can be lifted nearly clear of the ears, making fitting swift and without too much ear contact. The bit can then be attached to the cheekpiece on one side, encouraged into the mouth and attached to the cheekpiece on the other side. The reins are undone, pulled around either side of the horse's neck, and attached at the withers. If the horse does not accept this procedure, however careful the owner, holding his front leg up or creating a pull on his tail might just be enough to take his mind off his head long enough for the bridle to be fitted.

A clean pair of heels

SOLUTION Such behaviour requires a strict approach if someone is not to get hurt. A horse that turns his quarters on a person is threatening them, and such behaviour cannot be allowed. It may be possible to dodge round the horse and catch hold of him, but this is not addressing the problem. The range of a horse's hind legs is considerable, and his aim is usually spot on.

In order to teach the horse he will have to wear a headcollar at all times when in the stable. It should be fitted snugly, and there should be no protrusions in the stable on which he can catch it. The owner then arms him/herself with a pocketful of carrots and a long schooling whip, or a lungeing whip with the lash wound around it. On entering the stable, as soon as the horse attempts to swing his quarters round the owner must flick the whip at his quarters so that the horse feels it. He will probably take fright and jump into the corner, so the owner should be prepared for this. Alternatively the horse may jump around to face his owner, in which case the whip must be swiftly put

PROBLEM Some horses turn their quarters towards anyone who enters their stable, threatening to kick. Is there a particular reason for this behaviour and how can the horse be taught to face whoever enters the stable?

An owner using the carrot-and-stick method in the stable

BARGING

A horse that tries to barge or squash you against the wall is being downright bad-mannered, and such behaviour must not be tolerated. Firstly ensure the horse wears a headcollar at all times, so that you always have something to grab hold of immediately you enter the stable. Should he try to barge you, pull him hard towards you with the headcollar, flicking his hindquarters away so that he has to turn around you. Then give the command to stand. If you do this every time he tries to barge he will soon realise that he fails at every attempt, and should give up.

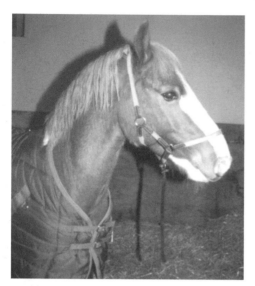

Note the short length of cord attached to the horse's headcollar. This will enable the owner to catch hold of the horse's head without the risk of a longer rope getting caught up in stable fittings

behind his/her back and a carrot produced for the horse. The owner then quickly takes hold of the headcollar and makes much of the horse. Sometimes it is a good idea to leave a short length of cord (6–12 in) on the headcollar to make it easier to catch hold of it. If the horse remains in the corner, the whip should be used to encourage him to turn and face his owner, coupled with a verbal command to 'come'. Once the horse complies a carrot is offered.

Corrective treatment for this problem needs to be intensive. The owner should visit the stable many times during the day, repeating the procedure until eventually the horse learns to face his owner immediately he or she enters the stable and thus receives his reward.

Sometimes the whip treatment won't work because the horse refuses to turn and face you. Another method is to corn-feed the horse by hand – that is, the owner holds the bucket whilst the horse eats. It may be necessary to give him six to seven feeds a day like this, a handful at a time. For the first two to three days it is as well not even to try and touch him, but just let him get used to your presence until he comes up for his feed calmly and happily. He may be kicking like this because he has been beaten up and abused in some way, and is really downright scared of people. So try to gain his trust, and don't bully and whip him even more.

Stroppy at shows

PROBLEM Why do some horses misbehave when at shows while others seem to take it all in their stride, and what can be done to make the stroppy horse behave?

SOLUTION It is not unusual for horses who are perfectly well behaved at home to misbehave when out at shows. Generally this is due to nerves and excitement, so in order to calm a stroppy horse down the cause of the excitement or worry needs to be established. Causes can include:

- coming into contact with others, when normally a horse lives alone;
- an excitable nature;
- an owner who is too lenient;
- overfeeding, or incorrect feeding for the type of horse;
- overfacing a young horse.

Where a horse lives alone, it is obvious that he will become excitable when in company. Horses are social herd animals, and keeping them alone is very unnatural for them. The solution is to provide a companion for the horse at home, and failing that, he should be taken out in the company of other horses as much as possible. Simply being allowed to walk around at a show for some time, before being expected to perform, will probably help him settle.

A horse with an excitable nature can be very difficult to keep calm. Calming supplements may help, such as camomile or brewers' yeast, or one of the wide choice of calming herbal formulations sold by herbal feed companies; and again, taking him out for as many 'jollies' as possible will help to show him that really shows are not such exciting places after all.

When an owner is too lenient, a horse will probably display bolshy behaviour. Often this can be the result of the owner not wanting to reprimand the horse in public for fear of being criticised – but this attitude helps no one. A horse is too large an animal to have prancing about in an uncontrolled way, but if he learns that he is never reprimanded when away from home he will start to do as he likes. The solution is to ensure that the horse is told off effectively the moment he misbehaves. The reprimand should be unpleasant but harmless, such as an instant stinging slap under the belly as soon as he tries to take advantage. On the first occasion he may be quite shocked, but he will soon learn that his owner has taken control.

A horse that is overfed, or incorrectly fed (perhaps being given too much heating food), will often feel really well in himself to a point where he starts to jump about and fidget. The solution is to cut the feed down, or to adjust it so that there is less heating food in the diet; for example if the horse is on competition cubes he should be put on to horse and pony cubes or a 'non-heating' diet.

Finally, it is quite easy to 'overface' a horse, even if you are only taking him to a local show. There are many unusual sights and sounds at shows – trade stands, loudspeakers, crowds, flags and so on – all of them a quite unnatural sight to a horse, and he needs time to adjust. Allowing him to look round a show without competing, for a few times if necessary, will be of lasting benefit to both horse and owner.

A horse misbehaving at a show while in-hand; such behaviour could easily lead to the owner being kicked or trampled

Nasty nipping

PROBLEM Some horses seem to feel that nipping is good fun. However, it is never a good idea to reprimand horses by smacking them on the nose, so how can such horses be punished without making them head-shy?

SOLUTION There are two possible solutions to this problem. Obviously hitting the horse round the head is not at all advisable as he will soon become head-shy. However, something unpleasant must happen to him immediately he nips so that he associates nipping with discomfort. One solution is immediately to jerk the whiskers around his muzzle every time he attempts to nip. Most horses detest this, and will soon stop nipping once they associate the unpleasant feeling every time they do it.

An alternative approach is always to have a metal or stiff plastic curry comb in the hand while carrying out any tasks around the horse. By keeping a close eye on the horse's movements, the owner will soon be able to recognize subtle changes in the horse's manner which generally indicate that a nip is about to be delivered. As soon as the horse brings his head forwards attempting to nip, the curry comb is put in his way and the horse will simply bite the metal or plastic. He will not like this one bit and will soon learn to associate the spiky feel of the curry comb with his own actions.

Planting the feet

PROBLEM Why do some horses refuse to lift up their feet for picking out or shoeing, and how can the problem be remedied?

CAUSE The horse is either plain stubborn, or else he has simply never been taught to pick up his feet when required, an essential lesson which should be part of every foal's routine training programme. Unfortunately many owners are simply too busy to repeat this lesson on a daily basis, and often the only time the horse has his feet picked up is when the farrier arrives. Having his feet trimmed therefore becomes an ordeal, and the young horse soon learns to associate picking his feet up with a problem. (While the act of trimming is not, in fact, unpleasant, the unfamiliarity of the event causes the horse some anxiety.)

SOLUTION Pick the horse's feet up as part of a daily routine. Start practising this while the horse is being fed, ie when he is occupied with something he likes. Run your hand down the horse's leg, apply a little pressure to the fetlock and give the command 'up'. The first few times the horse may not understand what is required and you may need to encourage him to lift his foot by leaning against his shoulder. This will encourage him to transfer his weight on to the opposite leg, thus making it easy for him to lift his foot. When carrying out this procedure with the hind feet, be careful; while most horses will not kick out, many will try to snatch their hoof from you, which may injure your hands or arms. If a horse does try to jerk his hoof backwards or forwards, simply hold fast. Try not to let go, unless you feel you are in danger. Otherwise the horse soon learns that he can evade having his feet picked up by snatching them away from you at every attempt. Once a horse complies with having his feet picked up he should be praised and you should guide the hoof back to the floor. Do not allow the horse to snatch his foot to the floor, or else this too can soon become a bad habit.

The stubborn horse poses quite a problem. Horses are far bigger and stronger than we are, so trying to prise a hoof from the floor is going to do nothing but give you big muscles! The stubborn horse must be made to realise that it is far more pleasant to pick his hoof up when requested than to leave it on the floor. Snatching at the feathers can often do the trick, as can applying more pressure than normal to the fetlock; however, a horse used to such tactics will not be persuaded to comply easily.

In order to make the horse lift his hoof you have to make his leg feel uncomfortable. To do this you can rub a mane comb along the bulbs of the heels, or put your thumb into the heel and apply pressure. Many horses will lift their foot up away from the uncomfortable sensation, and the minute they do this they should be praised. The hoof should be held for a few seconds and then guided to the floor. This can then be repeated four or five times with each foot in turn. Once the horse realises it is more comfortable for him to lift his hoof when requested than to keep it planted on the floor he should become a lot more amenable.

Vice prevention

SOLUTION There is great and continuing debate about the cause of vices; however, most experts agree that it is the horse's in-built urge to eat continually that plays the largest part in their development. In the wild, horses eat for about sixteen hours a day, consuming relatively low quality forage. As domesticated animals, however, they are now provided with better quality feed in an easily consumed form, and so generally get through their ration quickly, leaving plenty of time for more eating! This drives them to seek other ways of occupying themselves, and often this manifests itself in wood chewing, windsucking, crib-biting, weaving and so on.

In order to prevent such problems from occurring, the horse's food should be presented so as to make his eating time last longer. Hay should be fed in nets with very small holes so that he has to work quite hard for all that he gets, and his concentrates should be mixed with plenty of chaff and should be of a low enough nutritional quality that he can have a fair amount without becoming too fat. If the horse is turned out on his own in a field his concentrate ration can be spread over the floor so he has to search out every last grain or nut – though obviously food should never be scattered over wet, muddy soil.

Once vices are established they are extremely difficult, if not impossible to cure. Occupying the horse's time with the measures suggested above, and with other activities such as riding and grazing will help, but inevitably he will still carry out his habit in times of stress or boredom. Turn him out as much as possible in a field or paddock; this will often cure most vices, or at least reduce them, particularly in young horses.

While not cures, there are ways of stopping a horse from displaying these vices. For instance, crib-biters can be put in stables with flat walls, and in paddocks with electric fencing, and a metal strip put on the bottom stable half-door and any ledges. Weavers can have a weaving grille fitted to their stable, and those that chew wood can have foul-tasting liquid (such as bitter aloes or Cribox) applied to chewable surfaces. Unfortunately some horses will always find a way round these measures, and ultimately this is for the worse. Thus crib-biters can turn into windsuckers, weavers will continue their habit behind the grille, and those that chew wood find other things to chew, or start to windsuck! There are also several horse 'toys' on the market nowadays, although toys only work for those horses who have a desire to play with them. While a horse may be quite happy to chew a post, it does not necessarily follow that he will play with a toy instead. The best results come from introducing such toys to foals, who then tend to play with them throughout their first few years of life.

In short, the answer is to occupy the horse's time for as much as possible, and to remove anything that will help perpetuate his vice. He should be turned out as much as possible. Ultimately, however, a vice may have to be managed, rather than cured.

PROBLEM Many horses of differing temperaments develop stable vices of varying degrees. Why is this and can such vices be cured, or is it simply a case of having to live with them?

Nut-release feeders help to keep a horse occupied for hours, and so effectively emulate his natural eating behaviour

Windsucking

PROBLEM Windsucking is a vice that requires no 'props' in order for the horse to carry out the habit. Is there anything that he can wear to prevent him from doing it, and does the vice have any long-term health risks?

CAUSE Windsucking is a habit whereby the horse arches his neck, swallows in air and makes a rather peculiar gulping noise. The consequence of windsucking is that the stomach can become full of air – this is undoubtedly why the horse starts the habit in the first place, to give his stomach a 'full-up' feeling. This can lead to a horse becoming a 'poor doer' –he that never looks in good condition – or to frequent bouts of colic, or to a number of digestive disorders.

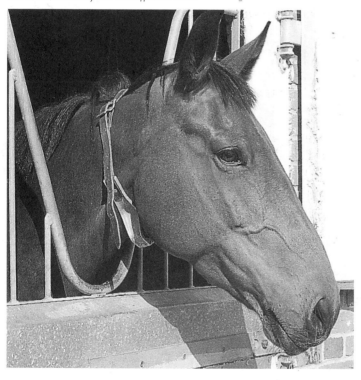

Anti-windsucking collars can help to prevent the habit, but they do not effect a cure

SOLUTION As explained on the previous page, the horse's time needs to be taken up as much as possible with other activities; when he is in the stable, however, there is a device that he can wear called a cribbing collar, or cribstrap. This is a leather strap that has two shaped metal sections that look a little like a large nutcracker. This fixes under the horse's throat at the point where the head meets the neck, and its purpose is to prevent the horse from arching his neck and thus being able to suck in air. It can work quite well, but does have to be fitted quite tightly in order to be effective.

The horse should be allowed periods where he does not wear the cribbing collar if he is not to become sore, and the strap should be kept clean and supple, the metal arms must also be kept perfectly clean. In the majority of cases a cribbing strap does work while fitted, although some horses can still persist with the habit in spite of wearing a collar. A cribbing collar is not a cure, merely a preventative. As with any vice, once the deterrent has been removed, the horse will resume the habit.

Door knocker!

PROBLEM Horses that kick their stable door can drive everyone in a yard mad! What can be done to prevent a horse from doing this, and can such behaviour cause the horse permanent damage?

SOLUTION The habit of door-kicking is a very difficult one to stop, or even to prevent. One of the biggest problems is that in order to quieten such a horse, he is usually given his feed, or given some attention as soon as he starts to bang so as to stop him. This is actually *rewarding* the horse for kicking the door, and encourages him to do it more and more! The first step in combating this problem is therefore to ignore the horse totally, no matter how annoying the noise gets. Over a period of weeks, or even months (ear plugs may be needed for all staff!), he will gradually realise that he is no longer being rewarded for displaying his habit, and with the incentive removed, it is possible that he may lose interest altogether and give up. Unfortunately, however, this is not always the case.

Once a horse starts to kick a door he becomes aware that it is the sound that brings people running. Another tactic that can therefore be employed is to pad the door with dense foam, or hessian sacks filled with straw. This reduces the noise and again proves a disincentive. It also has the benefit of protecting the horse's knee which can become damaged through kicking.

In good weather a sturdy breast-rail can be fitted to the door so that the horse cannot escape from his stable, but has nothing to kick against.

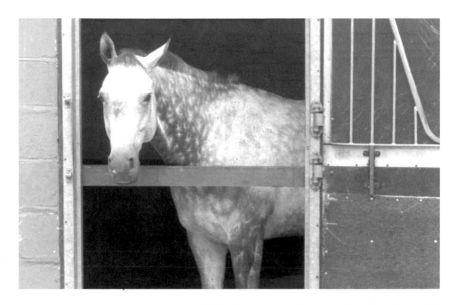

Placing a strong breast-rail across the stable doorway means that the horse has nothing to kick against

Pulling back

SOLUTION Tying up a horse is a point of discipline taken so much for granted that many people do not realise what a real problem it can be if a horse will not tie up until they experience it for themselves. However, a distinction needs to be made here between the young horse which has never really been taught to tie up, and an older horse that has realised that he can get free by pulling back and breaking the string.

With the young horse, patience and education are required. To start with the horse should be held with his quarters turned towards a wall: if he tries to pull back he will only be able to take a step or two before the wall, acting as a physical barrier, prevents him from doing so. When the horse moves back he should be held firmly by the head-collar and the verbal command 'Stand' should be said loudly and positively. Any disobedience such as trying to rear or pull away should be dealt with firmly. The head must be held tightly and the horse reprimanded for any unacceptable behaviour. However, praise should be given at every opportunity when the horse does well.

Another method for the youngster is 'reeling in': a lungeing rein is attached to the headcollar as normal (with the clip facing downwards), and the other end is placed through a tie-ring attached to a solid surface that will not give way under pressure, and held in the owner's hand. No breakable string should be used. Routine tasks such as grooming can be carried out with the free hand and as soon as the horse attempts to pull back the lunge rein is allowed to go slack – finding that he has nothing to pull against, he stops. The owner

PROBLEM Allowing himself to be tied up without pulling back is a lesson that a horse should learn early on in his life. What can be done to restrain him from pulling back uncontrollably if he has been allowed to get away with it for a period of time?

Firstly the youngster is patted and reassured (note the lunge line running through the tie-ring back to the handler)

The handler (out of shot to the left) then employs the reeling-in method until the horse has accepted that he must not pull back when tied up

then 'reels' the horse back in until he is standing close to the wall again. Every time the horse is required to tie up, this procedure should be used and within days he usually forgets all about pulling back and accepts being tied. At this point a breakable piece of string should be used. This is a good method for most horses as it not associated with any discomfort or rough handling.

The older horse which is confirmed in this habit will prove far more tricky. Firstly, a broad leather strap about 6in (15cm) in diameter can be put round the horse's neck a quarter of the way down his neck from the poll. Attached to this should be a strong metal ring that will not pull out under pressure; the horse should be tied from this strap. Once he feels the pressure he will try to pull back, but many horses thoroughly dislike pressure on their necks and so cease their pulling.

Should this fail, a lunge line around the quarters can be tried. The lunge line should be tied to the ring with a quick release knot as usual, then passed through the headcollar ring, down the horse's side around his hind thighs, back along his other side and attached to the headcollar ring. When he tries to pull back a forwards pressure will be put on his hind thighs, encouraging him to move forwards. The owner or handler should always be ready to give the command to stand, and to give an instant reprimand or reward as appropriate.

All these approaches should be attempted in a safe, confined area, and the handler should be on hand to free the horse in an emergency. However, he should not be too quick to interfere. Often people become scared when they see a horse struggling, but without the struggle the horse cannot learn to accept restraint.

TIP

It is a matter of discretion on the owner's part whether these methods are tried through 'reeling' or direct tying. Direct tying brings the quickest and most satisfactory results, but is not always suitable for a highly strung horse known to panic easily. For such a horse, the reeling method should be tried until he has learned to stand on command and accept pressure through the lead rein.

Basic stable safety

PROBLEM How can you ensure that you provide your horse with as safe a stabled environment as possible?

SOLUTION Firstly the horse's stable needs to be assessed to see what 'potential' hazards there are. Generally the more fixtures and fittings there are the more possibilities of damage to the horse.

Light switches are a common hazard. Watertight safety switches should be installed if the stable does not already have them. These should be sited outside the stable, where the horse cannot reach over and chew them; similarly, light bulbs must be protected in case your horse decides to try and eat them! A bulkhead fitting will give a good source of light inside a stable. Exterior power outlets should have safety covers.

Feed and water fittings should be kept to a minimum, as they only clutter up the stable, making it less safe. A manger should be of the removable corner type or one which fits over the door, so it can be removed for cleaning. A corner manger should be fitted in the front corner of a stable, away from the door, so that when you enter or leave the stable the horse is most likely to be standing with his hind legs away from you.

Horses which constantly knock their water over are a nuisance, so it may be necessary to use a wall bracket which holds the bucket. This should be hinged to fold flat when the bucket is taken out. Alternatively the water bucket can be put into an old tyre to aid stability. Automatic watering bowls are suitable for horses, but they need to be checked frequently, and kept free from hay or food.

Haynets should be tied up high enough so that the horse cannot get his foot caught in the holes. Hayracks are safe, but are less desirable as little bits of hay may fall into the horse's eyes. Many people simply feed hay off the floor in the corner. This is of course safe, but can also be rather wasteful.

Salt-lick holders are safe while they contain a new salt lick, but once the horse licks the salt block down the edges protrude and provide the horse with something to catch himself on. It is far safer to put an extra tie-ring into the stable wall and tie a salt lick (the type with a hole in the middle) onto this.

Stable tools should be kept away from horses or children. A specific storage area should be designated, to which all tools are returned to after use and positioned properly; forks or rakes lying about on the floor are simply waiting for someone to tread on them.

Doors and windows

Stable doors should be wide and high enough to allow a horse to pass through without injuring himself. A horse which rushes in or out of his stable has probably already knocked himself because the opening is too narrow or too low, and so has become nervous. The following are minimum guidelines for doorway measurements:

Width: 3ft 7in (1.1m)
Height of doorway: 7ft (2.1m)
Height of lower door: 4ft 2in (1.27m)

Doors should always open outwards; should the bedding pile up behind an inwards-opening door access to the stable could become difficult, which could be dangerous in an emergency. Two bolts should secure the lower door. In the event that the horse undoes the top one the bottom one will prevent him from escaping. Lower kick bolts (operated by the foot) save you bending down to open the door, and so save time in an emergency.

Windows should have a top vent which opens inwards and upwards to provide ventilation, but prevent draughts. They should be covered with galvanised mesh, or protected by iron bars, for safety.

ELECTRICITY SUPPLY

As most stable fires are started through electrical faults, this is an area which needs special consideration. All electrical installations should only be carried out by an approved contractor, who will ensure your requirements comply with present regulations. Any newly installed cabling should be well out of reach of any horse. It should also be waterproof, of a type which uses galvanised steel conduit or Mineral Insulated Cable (MICV) with a PVC covering.

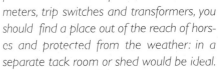

When choosing a site for the master switch panel, meters, trip switches and transformers, you should find a place out of the reach of horses and protected from the weather: in a separate tack room or shed would be ideal.

Any electrical appliances should also be checked regularly; this includes kettles and radios, as well as clippers or electric groomers. Existing electricity cables and equipment should be regularly checked for signs of wear. Common faults include:

a) loose plug wires - if you can see individual wires, rather than the usual thick PVC covering, rewire the plug as soon as possible
b) wires chewed by mice or rats
c) wires cracked through old age
d) split plugs and sockets
e) signs of overheating on plugs and sockets

Remember that horses are much more susceptible to fatal electrocution than humans. All stable-yard circuits should therefore be used with a life-saving Residual Current Device (RCD), which should be permanently wired into the circuit at the fuse box. An RCD is normally rated to operate at 30mA (30 thousandths of an amp), and in less than half a second it will break the circuit and switch everything off if there is a fault anywhere in the wiring.

Dust allergies

PROBLEM It is well known that straw beds can cause dust allergies in horses. Why is this, and are there alternative forms of bedding that are just as effective and just as economic?

TIP

A stable should never be mucked out while a horse is still in it. He should be turned out, tied up outside, or put in another box for at least half an hour after mucking out and laying the new bed has been finished. Also, ensure the horse's stable is really well ventilated. This prevents odours accumulating, and the constantly changing air will help to keep dust levels to a minimum.

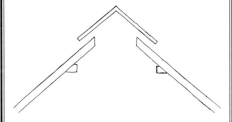

An open ridge stable roof with a protective cowl gives good air circlation

---

SOLUTION Straw is an exceptionally good bedding for horses because they can rummage about in it and this keeps them happy for hours, thus helping to prevent vices. However, some horses can develop allergies which can result in COPD (chronic obstructive pulmonary disease). While straw is blamed for many cases of COPD there are quite a few other sources of stable dust and fungal spores which can cause the disease. These include:

■ **Mouldy or dusty hay**
Only clean hay should be fed, and it may help to steam or soak the hay of a hyper-sensitive horse. Hay that has been soaked should be consumed overnight, and the remainder discarded in the morning.

■ **Agricultural sprays and waste blown in off the fields**
The effects of such sprays are not fully understood, but some horses do suffer asthma-like symptoms when fields in a close proximity are being sprayed. Farmers should be asked to notify local owners when spraying so that horses can be kept in away from the area.

■ **Dust from neighbouring stables**
This can be a real problem. It is a waste of time to eradicate dust in one horse's stable, if those next to him are still enduring dusty environments. In a livery yard the horse with an allergy should be moved to a box where a completely dust-free environment can be established.

■ **Dusty feeds**
There really is no excuse for dusty feeds. Only good quality forage should be purchased, and it should be stored in a cool, dry place and used by its sell-by date.

■ **Deep-litter beds**
Deep-litter beds can cause quite severe allergic reactions, as mould develops in the bed releasing spores which are then inhaled into the horse's respiratory system.

Dust-free bedding alternatives include dust-extracted wood shavings; chopped, dust-extracted straw; and peat and paper bedding. All have their advantages and disadvantages, so using one sort as opposed to another is purely down to personal preference. For instance, dust-extracted wood shavings can take a while to 'bed down', and the quality can vary from batch to batch; however, once the bed is established they are quick and economical to manage. Chopped, dust-extracted straw can be quite appetising to horses despite what the manufacturers say, so it is not always a good choice for those which are greedy. Peat bedding is excellent as a bed, in that it keeps the horse warm and cosy, but it often leaves his coat looking quite messy, and it can become compacted in his hooves. Paper bedding can take quite a while to bed down, and it needs to be skipped out frequently or it can become quite soggy. All of these are more expensive than straw; however, if the cost of veterinary care and the risk to a horse's health are weighed up against the monetary savings, then an alternative bedding often proves worthwhile.

Waving goodbye to winter woollies

SOLUTION Unfortunately there is no miracle solution to make the horse shed his coat quickly. All horses moult differently, some taking a matter of days to shed their whole coat, others taking weeks and weeks! It is important that the horse is not allowed to become cold, as this will encourage him to hold on to his coat; he should therefore be well rugged up, especially after exercise if that is what he is used to.

No amount of force can prise the coat from the horse's skin, but a rubber curry comb, or metal hair scraper, will pull out all the loose hair. The addition of cod liver oil to the feed at this time will help to establish a sleek coat as it comes through.

PROBLEM It is a fact of life that a horse will moult during the early spring, covering all who groom him with mounds of hair that is impossible to remove from clothing! Is there any way of removing the coat painlessly but quickly, or does the horse owner simply have to be resigned to being covered in hairs for weeks?

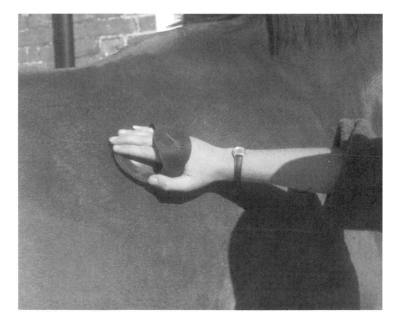

A rubber curry comb, used in circular movements, will help to dislodge the moulting hair

Warning

A horse should never have a sheet of polythene placed between his coat and his rug in order to 'make him sweat it out', this is an 'old wives' tale and does nothing more than cause him extreme discomfort. The excessive sweating that may occur could prove quite damaging to him, possibly causing skin allergies and predisposing him to catching a chill.

TIP

A horse that is known to keep hold of his heavy winter coat for some months can be clipped without detriment. The summer coat will not be spoiled as some people might think, and such clipping will benefit the horse by making him more comfortable. The best time to clip for this purpose is around late February or early March.

Sensitive skin

PROBLEM A dislike of grooming in well bred, fine-coated horses is fairly common. Why should this be so, and what can be done to encourage the horse to enjoy his grooming sessions more?

SOLUTION A dislike of grooming in any horse usually stems from rough treatment in the past. A horse may show this dislike in a number of ways ranging from restlessness, biting or kicking, and pulling back on the lead-rope. The solution lies in restoring the horse's trust in his owner, and in regaining his confidence in relation to the grooming activity. This can be done by:

- *not* scrubbing at sensitive areas such as the head and belly with a hard brush;
- *not* banging his body or joints with the back of a brush;
- making sure he knows where the person grooming is at all times. Sudden movements will only make him jumpy;
- using a soothing voice;
- *not* using a metal or plastic curry comb on his body;
- rubbing ticklish areas with the hand or a stable rubber to remove any mud or dirt;
- using the fingers to untangle knots in the mane and tail, rather than pulling at either with a curry or mane comb;
- offering him a haynet to chew on while being groomed.

The important thing is not to go too fast – the horse himself should dictate the pace. Some will only tolerate a few minutes of grooming, others are more accepting, even if they are sensitive. Grooming should be done gently but efficiently, and the time spent on the activity should be built up over a number of weeks until the horse tolerates being groomed for an adequate period of time, eventually he may accept it completely, and even begin to enjoy it!

The benefits of banging

PROBLEM Does 'banging' (traditionally known as strapping) with a wisp, stable rubber or leather strapping pad, really help to improve a horse's muscles and top line?

SOLUTION Banging certainly can help to improve the horse's physique, but it can only help to enhance what is already there: it will not make a thin horse look fatter, not will it improve faults in conformation.

Banging should be introduced steadily and gradually until the horse becomes used to the sensation. As the pad is bought down towards the horse he will anticipate the 'thump' that follows. This causes him to contract his muscles in order to resist the pressure. In turn this tones the muscles and therefore builds them up. Only well padded areas should be worked upon, such as the rump, neck, shoulders and hind thighs. Bony parts such as the ribs, back and hips should be avoided. If the horse seems to dislike the activity, it may be that the strokes applied by the person strapping are too heavy or vigorous, and he will need to use a gentler approach. It is often easier to use two pads, one in each hand so that a rhythmic pattern can be achieved.

Areas which can safely be worked on

Improving the coat

SOLUTION Some horses do seem to have better coats than others, and often for no apparent reason. The first necessity is to ensure that the horse is being fed correctly and groomed sufficiently. Once this is established, cod liver oil can be added to the horse's feed which will help to bring out a shine. This is especially effective at those times of year when the coat is changing. How warm the horse is will also affect his coat: thus if he is cold, his coat will look starey and dull, so rugs may be required to keep him warmer. Worming also plays a part in the condition of the coat, as a horse carrying a high worm burden will often have a dull, dry coat. The horse's teeth should also be checked, because if he is not masticating his food properly, he may not be deriving maximum benefit from it.

PROBLEM Some horses never seem to have a shine to their coats no matter how much they are groomed. Why is this, and what can be done to improve a coat's appearance?

TIP

If a horse is destined for the show ring, extra attention should be paid to the glossiness of his coat. The elements of sun and rain can damage the coat, so a light New Zealand rug, or a summer sheet may be necessary to keep the coat lying flat and sleek and to maintain its richness of colour.

If your horse has a dull, listless coat, first check his diet and grooming regime to make sure that he is receiving the right attention - both inside and out!

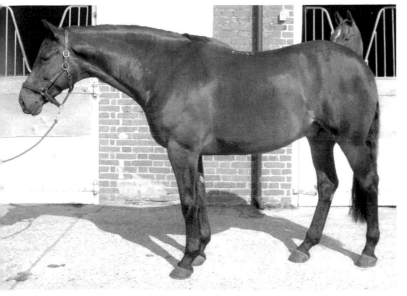

Extra 'bloom' can be obtained by adding oil to the horse's feed, and by being vigilant with grooming and rugging as appropriate for the time of year

Careful cleaning

PROBLEM

Do a horse's genitals need cleaning, and if so, how exactly can this be accomplished without the handler getting kicked? Additionally, what products should be used so as not to make the horse sore?

TIP

Baby wipes are an excellent addition to the grooming kit, providing a quick, sensitive wipe on a daily basis, when time is of the essence.

SOLUTION

A horse's genitals do require cleaning, although some horses appear not to become as dirty as others. This may be due to the conformation of the individual's genital areas, or to other factors such as the horse's environment. In general, mares tend to become dirtier than geldings, especially when they are in season. The dock and vulva should be kept clean as a part of routine grooming. Warm water and a sponge are all that is needed, and the area should simply be sluiced down; once clean, it should be dried and kept supple by applying a little baby oil. A mare's udders should be treated in the same way.

A gelding can prove a little more difficult as his sheath comprises many folds of skin when his penis is tucked up inside. The easiest way to clean a gelding's sheath is to apply a sheath-cleaning gel, or baby oil, as far into the folds as possible. This should be left on for a day or two and then sluiced out with warm water and a sponge. If the sheath has been allowed to become caked up, a few applications of gel may be needed before sluicing out will be of much benefit. A good indication of when a sheath is really dirty, is a sticky discharge down the back legs. Some geldings require their sheath to be cleaned very regularly, perhaps every week or fortnight, while others never seem to get dirty at all.

If a horse is very sensitive it may take a lot of patience and tact before he or she allows his or her genitals to be cleaned without a fuss.

Washing a gelding's sheath: the application of sheath gel, baby oil or petroleum jelly a few days before cleaning will help to soften the mucky deposits in the folds of the skin

(Far right) After a few days the sheath can be sluiced out gently by using a sponge and some warm water

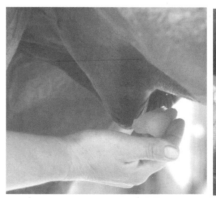
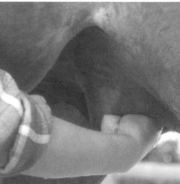

A mare's udder requires regular cleaning as part of the overall grooming routine

(Far right) Baby wipes are a great help for quick results on a daily basis

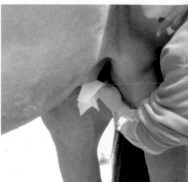

Washing worries

SOLUTION Rinsing a sweaty horse off after exercise is fine, providing he has been walked for the last mile or so and therefore arrives at the yard with his muscles relaxed. During the summer months it is quite all right to use water straight from the tap, but the horse must have any excess water removed from his coat with a sweat scraper. A brisk rub over with a towel will also help to get the circulation going. The horse can then be safely turned out into the paddock, so that he can roll and relax; in mild, warm weather there is no likelihood of him catching a chill, and only a minimal amount of his natural oils will be lost by rinsing with plain water.

The winter does pose a problem. If a horse with a long coat is left wet in cold conditions he is very likely to suffer, not only because he may become severely chilled, but also due to the possible development of problems such as arthritis of the spine which can occur over a period of time, and kidney and liver complaints. If the horse has arrived home calm, then the dried sweat should simply be brushed off. But what about the excitable horse that comes home dripping wet, no matter how much he is walked for the last part of the ride? (See also Excessive sweating page 31.)

In this case the horse should be taken into a stable, or at least shielded from any wind, and quickly rinsed with warm water; all the excess water must be removed with a sweat scraper, and he should be rubbed briskly with a towel. He can then have an anti-sweat rug put on, with another warmer rug over the top; this causes a layer of air to be trapped between the horse's skin and the top rug which helps to dry him off. Once he is dry the anti-sweat rug must be removed if he is not to overheat and break out into a sweat again. Drying in this way usually takes between forty and fifty minutes, so time should be allowed for this in the horse's routine.

PROBLEM Most horses sweat when ridden, even if it is just under the saddle. Can a horse be washed down after a ride to remove this sweat, or will this take the natural oils out of his coat? Also, is it acceptable to use cold water, or should only hot water be used?

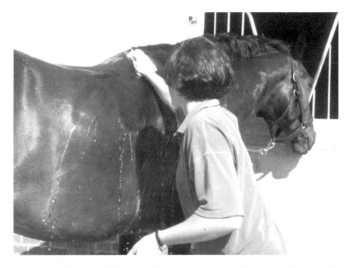

(Above) Sponging the saddle area after a ride will help to cool and refresh the horse
(Below left) In cold weather a horse should be quickly towel-dried after rinsing off to prevent him catching a chill
(Below) If the horse has sweated profusely, he should be washed down and then thatched with straw under a rug, as shown, and kept in the stable until he has dried off

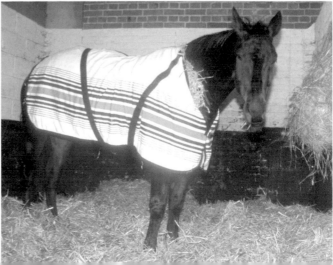

Baggy plaits

PROBLEM   When plaiting a tail it is easy for it all to end up baggy and lumpy. How can a tail be plaited so that it looks smart enough for the show ring, yet is easy enough to accomplish?

TIP

When intending to plait a tail it should be washed about a week beforehand to allow the oils to re-establish themselves and so give the hair some grip – a newly washed tail is too slippery to handle. The application of some baby oil on the lower half of the tail will help to give it a shine and keep it tangle free.

Step-by-step:

1. In order to plait a tail it must have been left to grow naturally at the top for at least six months. A thick tail looks lovely when plaited, but it also takes some practice if the end result is not to look clumsy.

2. The tail should be combed so there are no knots to obstruct the plaiting process.

3. To help keep the hairs together, the top of the tail should be dampened with water and a water brush.

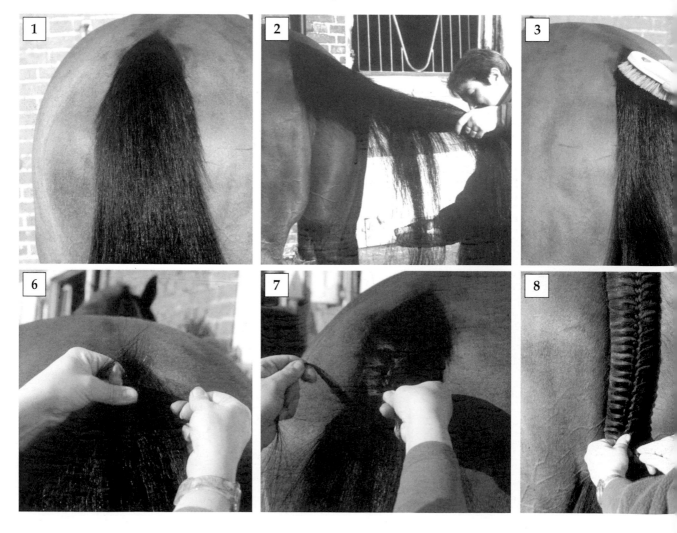

[4] A thin section of hair should be taken from either side of the top of the tail, and from the very centre of the top of the tail.

[5] The left section should be taken over the top of the middle one and pulled taut.

[6] The right section should then be taken across the middle section to the left and pulled taut.

[7] The plait should be continued in this way, ensuring that narrow, even sections are taken at a time and pulled tight to the dock.

[8] Once the end of the dock bone has been reached the plait can be finished off: do not take in any more sections, but continue to plait down with the hair already taken into the plait.

[9] The end of the long plait can be secured with a rubber band (the same colour as the tail hair) or with a needle and thread.

[10] The plait is finished by looping the end up underneath the point where the dock plait ended, and is then sewn into place. The loop can either be left, or sewn together depending on personal preference.

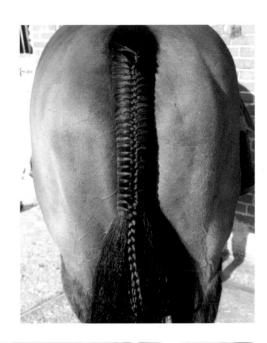

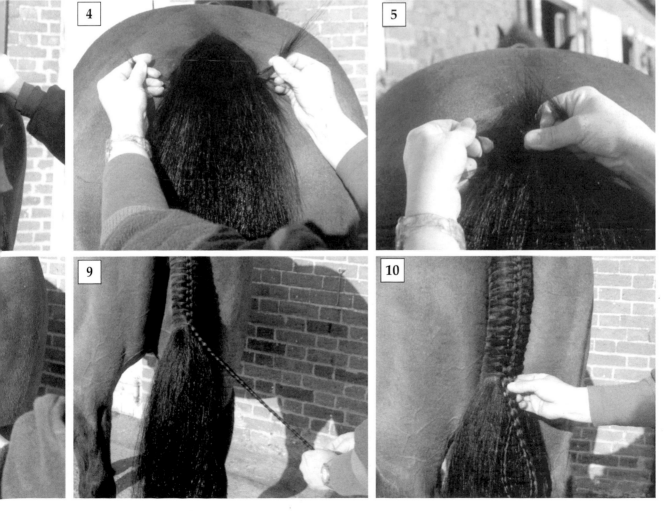

RIDGED PLAIT

A ridged plait is a reversed tail plait, where the plait appears to sit on top of the dock rather than smooth to it. To accomplish a ridged plait, steps 1 to 4 on the previous page should be followed. Then steps 5 and 6 should read:

5 *The left section should be taken under the middle one and pulled taut.*

6 *The right section should then be taken to the left under the middle section and pulled taut.*

Then continue with steps 7 to 10.

A ridged tail plait (right) is more prominent than the ordinary tail plait (far right)

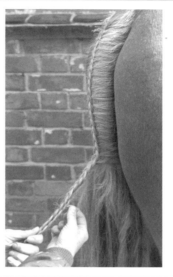
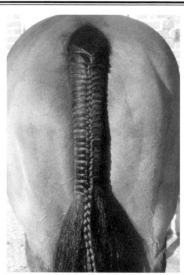

Pulling problems

PROBLEM Why do some horses seem to detest having their manes pulled whilst others accept it quite happily?

Using a razor comb to trim and shorten a horse's mane is a more humane method than the traditional one involving a mane comb – a more pleasant experience for both horse and owner!

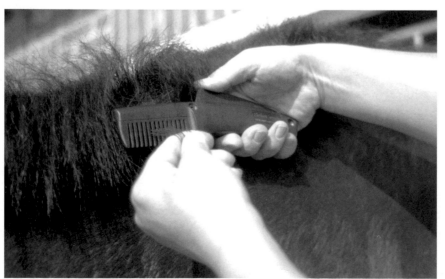

SOLUTION Many traditionalists are of the opinion that mane and tail pulling does not hurt a horse. However, if he resents having it done, then it must be causing him some discomfort, or at least he has suffered discomfort in the past when his mane or tail were pulled. It is true that some horses are more sensitive than others, but some owners are also more skilful than others and cause their horse the minimal amount of suffering. The question has to be asked whether pulling manes and tails is an essential part of turnout. The answer is that it is not, and that there are alternatives. If the horse does not need to be plaited up in the conventional way for showing, his mane can be left long, and a running plait used to keep it tidy and out of the way if and when necessary. If however, the mane *does* need to be plaited for shows, then a thinning comb can be used to thin and shorten the mane in readiness for plaiting. These are like a normal comb but have a razor blade in the centre which is activated at the point where the mane is to be shortened. Used with care, a presentable appearance can be achieved without causing the horse distress.

If there really is no alternative to pulling (perhaps because a horse has such a coarse mane that using a thinning comb leaves it too stubbly to plait) then the fingers should be used to pull out just a few – a *very* few – hairs at a time. This will take quite a long time to achieve, and the owner should plan to accomplish it over a week or so, rather than days. If a horse is treated in this caring way, he will lose his fear of having his mane or tail pulled over a period of time.

No tail

PROBLEM

What can be done to improve a horse's tail when it has been rubbed, chewed or is generally wispy?

SOLUTION

If a horse's tail is being rubbed, the cause must be identified and eradicated before any action can be taken to improve its appearance. If it is due to flies or sweet itch, then these problems must be treated with appropriate topical solutions such as citronella as a fly repellent, and benzo benzoate or some such proprietary application to soothe sweet itch irritation (see also page 120). If the tail is being chewed by other horses, then foul-tasting solutions used for horses that crib-bite can be applied to the tail to discourage this.

Obviously it will take a long while for the tail to grow back, so what can be done in the meantime? It is possible to purchase false tails and these are very good; they anchor to the existing tail and create a totally natural look as long as a good colour match can be found. If one of these tails cannot be obtained, it is possible to make one by acquiring tail hair from an abattoir. This can then be sewn into the existing hair to create a fuller look. Obviously, such measures will not be necessary for the everyday riding horse, but they can make a great difference to the appearance of horses in the show ring.

*(Below left) A thin, wispy tail detracts from a horse's appearance, and can cause him to lose that extra 'sparkle' needed in the show ring
(Centre) A somewhat extreme example of the full appearance which can be achieved in the addition of a false tail
(Right) False tails come in an array of colours and lengths to suit most horses and ponies*

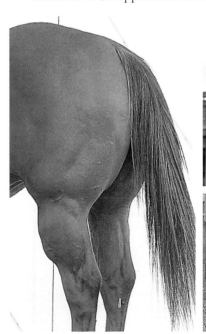

Clipper-phobic

PROBLEM

As winter approaches many owners dread the thought of clipping their horse, or having him clipped, and some horses really do seem to have a phobia about clipping. Why is this, and what can be done to clip him in safety, and with the least fuss and distress to the horse?

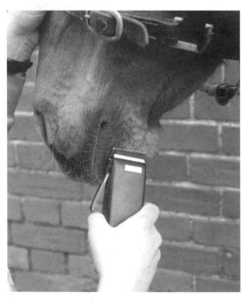

A sensitive horse will often tolerate small, hand-held clippers around his head

SOLUTION

The root of this problem again usually lies in poor early management of the horse: an uncaring, or uneducated approach when he was first clipped may have left permanent unpleasant memories that prevent the horse from being able to stand good-naturedly for clipping.

Remedying the situation takes time and the utmost patience. At first the clippers should simply be rested against the horse while switched off. Then they should be moved all over his body so that he can get used to the look of them and the cable. Next, they should be taken some distance away from him and switched on. It is a good idea to leave them running outside the box on a table while the normal grooming routine is carried out. Gradually they can be brought nearer to the horse, but not put on him – and if he seems at all alarmed, the pace is too fast and the clippers should be moved further away. The horse should be reassured all the time, until finally the clippers can be placed onto his body; they should then be moved all over his skin surface without actually clipping any hair off. As the horse's acceptance of the situation dictates, clipping can start once he is quite happy with the noise and feel. This whole procedure may take days, weeks or months depending on the severity of the horse's dislike.

Playing soothing music such as Bach or Mozart may also help to calm the horse and distract his attention from some of the noise.

- Should the horse's phobia be so great that the above procedure does not effect a solution, physical restraints may be needed. Many people do not like to sedate a horse, but in all honesty this probably causes the horse the least amount of stress. Other alternatives include:
- using a twitch, but this should only be employed by someone knowledgeable who appreciates that it must be removed every twenty minutes to allow the circulation back into the horse's lip;
- clipping the horse with small, silent-running hand-held clippers if he will accept them. Using them will take some time, and even if he gradually learns to accept normal clippers for the main areas of his body, a small, silent pair may prove invaluable for sensitive areas such as the head, belly and between the hind legs.

TIP

Before any clipping is carried out the following checks should be made to ensure that:

- *the clipper blades are sharp, since blunt blades will pull on the horse's coat;*
- *the tension between the blades is correct;*
- *the blades and clippers are well oiled;*
- *the clippers are correctly earthed, and are attached to a circuit breaker;*
- *the horse is standing on a dry, non-slip surface.*

Whipping off whiskers

SOLUTION The long whiskers found around the horse's eyes and muzzle are indeed part of his sensory system. They help him to feel objects as well as alerting him that his face is coming into close contact with something; and they play a part when he is socialising and communicating with other horses by sniffing, nostril to nostril. They also help to a small extent in repelling flies from his face. However, there are really very few risks in the domesticated world of the horse: rubbish and dangerous objects are removed from paddocks, companions are well known, and responsible owners ensure that horses sensitive to flies are sprayed with fly repellent and wear fly fringes if necessary. Therefore clipping the whiskers is not going to affect the domesticated horse a great deal, so it is really a matter of preference. If the horse is not needed for the show ring, why bother? And if he is, then trimming will probably be necessary to create the 'streamlined' appearance that judges seem to like.

PROBLEM What is the purpose of a horse's whiskers? Are they there to help the horse feel, and if so, surely trimming them is to the horse's detriment?

A horse with untrimmed whiskers: the 'natural' look

Trimmed whiskers give an altogether more streamlined appearance

Excessive sweating

SOLUTION A minimal 'neck and belly' clip will help to prevent the thicker-coated horse from becoming so hot and bothered. This is achieved by removing a strip of coat from beneath the gullet, down the front of the neck and chest and a strip from beneath the belly; if possible, removing a little hair from between the hind legs will also help. The horse will still have plenty of hair to keep him warm while living out, and provided his rugs are deep enough and he has sufficient shelter, he should not suffer as a result of the clip.

Unless the horse is used for showing, there is no reason why he cannot also be clipped during the summer months if the weight of his coat still causes him to sweat. It may look a little odd at first, but it soon begins to blend in, and it is far better to have it off than to cause him distress, and for him to lose condition.

PROBLEM Many horses, especially those with native blood, have thick, hairy coats which can cause them to sweat up very easily when ridden or when they are excited, resulting in a loss of condition. As it is difficult to dry a sweaty, hairy coat without the risk of a chill it would seem a good idea to clip the horse, thus removing the problem. However, many native horses and ponies are kept out of doors most, if not all the time during the winter months, so how can their coats be clipped without causing them to feel the cold? And what can be done if such a horse fails to shed its coat properly during the summer months, resulting in an all-year-round sweating problem?

TIP

Do take care if clipping a horse's summer coat, as temperatures can fall dramatically after the heat of the day. Ensure that the horse is warm enough at all times by providing a light summer rug if it does turn a little chilly. He may also require a summer sheet in the daytime if his skin is sensitive to flies.

Faulty fitting

PROBLEM
A bit that is incorrectly fitted can cause all sorts of problems, from mouth sores, to a horse which rears or bolts. How is a bit measured, and how is a horse's mouth measured to ensure the fit is correct?

SOLUTION
A bit is measured along the mouthpiece from cheekpiece to cheekpiece, regardless of type. A horse's mouth is measured from the corner of the lips on one side, to the corner on the other. The easiest way to do this is to use a piece of string: a knot should be made in one end, which is then placed on the corner of the lips on one side; the string is placed over the tongue in the mouth and pulled taut to the other corner of the lips, where another knot is made. The measurement between the knots will provide the horse's mouth size; another $^3/_4$in needs to be added to this measurement to obtain the ideal bit size.

A bit which is too small will pinch the corners of the horse's mouth; this will lead to discomfort and ultimately sores

BITLESS BRIDLES

These can provide the answer to a number of bitting problems: where the horse has abnormal mouth or jaw conformation; where he has a sore mouth; where he has teeth problems, eg on a youngster who is teething, or a horse which has recently had dental treatment.

TIP

Bits are now sized in ¼in increments so it is possible to get exactly the right size for any horse. Different types of mouthpiece can measure slightly differently, so a bit needs to be fitted to each horse individually. If the wrong size of bit has been purchased, a saddlery should be happy to change it for the next size up or down.

How to measure a bit: remember that if the bit is too wide it will slide and bruise the mouth; if too narrow it may press the lips and cheeks against the teeth, and will cause pinching

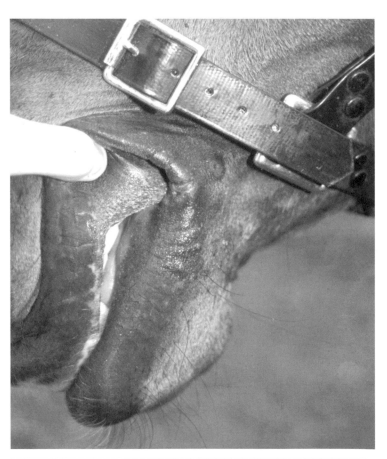

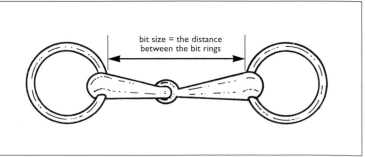

bit size = the distance between the bit rings

Pinching the corners

SOLUTION   A bit that is too small will be pulling against the cheeks of the horse's face and possibly wrinkling the skin as well, and it must be changed for a bigger one. Although the 'mouthpiece' of a bit may fit the horse well, the cheek-pieces can have an effect on the overall comfort of the bit. In general, bits with loose rings need to be chosen $^1/_4$in larger than those with eggbutt rings.

   If the bit fits perfectly but the horse still seems unhappy, it may be that his mouth conformation or his mouth movement is at fault and making things uncomfortable. In such a case, rubber bit guards may help; these pull over the bit and sit between the horse's cheek and the cheekpiece of the bit.

PROBLEM   What can be done if a bit seems to be pinching the corners of a horse's mouth?

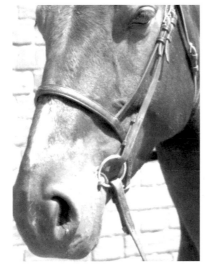

This bit is clearly too small, as evidenced by the wrinkled skin above the bit ring

Rollered mouthpieces

SOLUTION   The reason rollered mouthpieces are now considered adversely is because from the manufacturing point of view it became apparent that it was almost impossible to have the rollers close enough to each other so that they did not pinch the tongue. Furthermore, even if the bit *was* manufactured in an acceptable form, the rollers soon worked loose with use. Consequently the horse's tongue was pinched, if not more seriously injured, leaving permanent damage.
Alternatives include:
- using a mouthpiece that incorporates copper (not rollered) to help the horse salivate;
- using a straightbar mouthpiece, instead of a jointed one, for a horse that tries to grab hold of the mouthpiece;
- offering the horse that does not salivate a piece of apple just before mounting, or putting molasses onto the bit;
- using a flash noseband to prevent the horse opening his jaw and attempting to grab hold of the bit.

PROBLEM   Rollered mouthpieces used to be considered a good option for horses which did not salivate, or for horses which would grab hold of the mouthpiece. Now they are considered to be a bad thing by some manufacturers. Why is this and are there any alternatives?

Rollered mouthpieces are falling from favour because they can pinch the horse's tongue

Sticking out the tongue

PROBLEM Why do some horses stick their tongue out of the side of their mouth, and why do others hold their tongue between their teeth?

Where a horse holds his tongue between his teeth it should be established whether he has a mouth conformational defect or whether he is simply trying to evade his owner

SOLUTION There are two reasons for both these problems. The first is resistance on the horse's part – it is a form of evasion; the second is due to the horse's mouth conformation. Where the horse is simply trying to evade the bit, corrective schooling, together with fitting a flash noseband is the answer. Where the problem is a physical one, because the horse's mouth is of unusual conformation, the bit may need changing – for instance a horse with a fleshy tongue or a shallow palate may find it difficult to fit his tongue under the mouthpiece. A thinner mouthpiece or one specially designed to accommodate the fleshy tongue should be used. However, thinner mouthpieces are more severe, so be careful to ride sympathetically, particularly on the first few occasions. Again, a flash noseband may be required for a while to encourage the horse to realise that he does now have room for his tongue and the mouthpiece.

A horse that carries his tongue between his teeth may have a problem with his teeth – a veterinary surgeon, or dental specialist will be able to confirm this. Sometimes a horse's back teeth grow long, which results in the front teeth not being able to close together; this allows the tongue to slip through, and often the horse 'holds' it between his front teeth. Obviously the answer is to have the horse's teeth attended to. If no problem is found, the solution is the same as for the horse which sticks his tongue out of the side of his mouth.

Double jointed

PROBLEM What is the difference between a Dr Bristol and a French link, and why would you use one instead of the other?

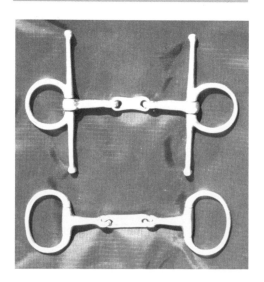

The French link bit (top left) is good for 'fussy mouthers', as it 'moulds' slightly to the shape of the horse's mouth. The Dr Bristol (below) suits many horses who do not respond to curb pressure

SOLUTION The mouthpieces of these bits vary in both their appearance and their action. While they are both members of the snaffle family, in a range of one to ten the French link rates about a one or a two in severity, while the Dr Bristol rates an eight or nine. Each of the bits has a 'link' in the middle: that of the French link is shaped like a flat peanut and lies flat in the horse's mouth. The Dr Bristol's link is larger and blunter with square edges, and lies at an angle to the roof of the horse's mouth.

The French link is useful for horses that require only mild pressure and a gentle action. Little pressure if any is put on the tongue, and the action on the corners of the mouth is gentle. Conversely the Dr Bristol is used for horses that require more pressure in order for the rider to keep control. This is one of the reasons it is often used for horses competing in cross country events. When the rider's hands are raised, quite severe pressure is directed onto the tongue, causing the horse to slow down.

Tongue over the bit

SOLUTION Some horses manoeuvre their tongues over the bit because incorrect bitting in the past has encouraged them to do so. It is an annoying and potentially dangerous habit – because rider control becomes minimal – and it should be prevented at all costs. Right from the start, when the horse is first bitted, care should be taken to ensure that the bit is exactly the right size and the right type, taking into consideration his age, mouth conformation and temperament. In addition the whole bridle should be correctly adjusted so that the horse is completely comfortable when wearing it.

PROBLEM Why do some horses get their tongue over the bit, and how can this annoying habit be prevented, if not cured altogether?

If the horse in question is an older horse which has been allowed to develop the habit, there are corrective measures that can be taken. First, the mouth should be checked for physical problems. In the absence of these, the type of bit should be considered. Take into account the horse's mouth conformation (see page 34), then consider the type of bit that might suit him best. If he seems to resent tongue pressure, a mullen or straightbar mouthpiece will be a better alternative to a jointed one as such mouthpieces spread the weight and action evenly across the tongue. The bit may need to be fitted a little higher than normal so that a definite wrinkle is seen at the corners of the lips. Remember that even if a different bit solves the cause of the problem, the horse will still need to learn that a) his mouth is no longer uncomfortable; and b) that putting his tongue over the bit is simply no longer possible. Only then will he settle in his mouth and forget all about putting his tongue over the bit.

TIP

More drastic measures may need to be taken with a horse that persists in getting his tongue over the bit. In such a case a tongue grid can be used. This is a fine, metal, W-shaped mouthpiece which is used in conjunction with the horse's normal bit. It sits on the tongue at the back of the mouth preventing the horse from drawing his tongue back towards his throat in order to get it over the mouthpiece.

A perfect fit

PROBLEM Whilst a saddle may have been an excellent fit initially, horses change shape, and so do saddles. How can you ensure that a horse won't suffer as a result of faulty fitting?

FITTING PROBLEMS

■ *Too much padding can cause a sore back, as the saddle will have a tendency to rock from side to side, causing friction points.*

■ *Flat padding endangers the spine, as the gullet can meet the back in extreme cases. Pressure points can also cause sores.*

■ *Too low at the pommel or too wide, and the withers will be rubbed.*

■ *If the padding is lumpy, then localised pressure points will cause sores and discomfort.*

■ *If the saddle looks as though it is perched on top of the back with the pommel extremely high above the withers, then the tree is too narrow. The gullet of any saddle should be 3in (7.6cm) wide all the way along.*

■ *If the saddle appears to swamp the horse, with the pommel very low at the wither, then the tree is too wide.*

SOLUTION Horses alter according to their work and condition – thus a fat horse can become slimmer, and vice versa; and a young horse will mature and change shape. As regards the saddles, the flocking inevitably becomes flatter with wear. Ensuring a correct fit is therefore an ongoing responsibility.

Initial fitting should be done by an expert, which in the UK would be a member of the Master Saddlers Association; however, it is necessary to know what to look for, so that potential problems can be spotted in the future. Many saddlers will bring quite a few saddles with them, so that if a first choice is not suitable, another can be selected. Before selecting a possible saddle he will measure the horse's back and will also assess his conformation, as poor conformation can dictate what type of saddle is most suitable. Most saddles come in narrow, medium or wide fittings. When fitting he will ensure that:

■ The tree of the saddle is the correct shape and width. If it is, then he can finely adjust the way the saddle sits by inserting or removing the flocking as necessary. This is known as 'setting up'.

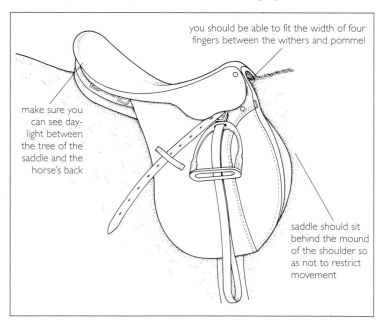

you should be able to fit the width of four fingers between the withers and pommel

make sure you can see daylight between the tree of the saddle and the horse's back

saddle should sit behind the mound of the shoulder so as not to restrict movement

■ Once fitted, there is no pressure on or near the spine, with or without a rider. Also that no weight is taken on the loins, but that it is evenly spread over the lumbar muscles.

■ The saddle sits even and level.

■ The pommel does not put any pressure on the withers either with or without a rider. Four fingers should be able to fit between the pommel and wither.

■ Daylight can be seen through to the withers when viewed from behind.

■ It does not restrict the horse's movement from the shoulder.

Ripping yarns

SOLUTION Rug-tearing is a very annoying and costly habit that comes in degrees from the odd rip to a horse tearing his rug to shreds overnight. The most obvious reasons for a horse doing this are:

- he is too hot and is trying to rid himself of the discomfort;
- he is trying to fill up his time because his feeding urge is not being satisfied (see also page 51);
- he is uncomfortable because the rug does not fit correctly.

Whatever the reason for its onset, once the habit has developed it is increasingly difficult to stop, even if the original cause is removed. The horse that is too hot is probably the easiest to cure, providing action is taken immediately he is seen to tear at his rug. First he should be felt under his rug to check that he is not too hot. If he does feel quite warm, his temperature should be taken to confirm whether he is, in fact, overheating. If he is sweating then quite obviously he is too hot. In such a case his rug either needs to be removed or changed for a lighter one, or one that is breathable (if the one he is already wearing is not).

PROBLEM Why do some horses tear at their rugs, and what can be done to stop them?

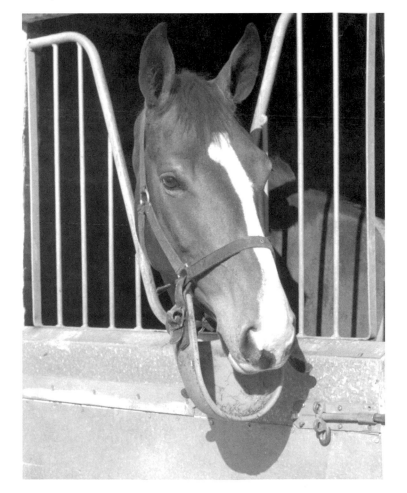

A bib can prevent a horse from undressing himself and tearing his rug to shreds

A horse that is trying to fill out his 'eating time' should be provided with a continuous supply of hay and should be allowed to occupy himself in other activities; for example he could be turned out for long periods if at all possible, otherwise stable toys may help to occupy his time, rather than his rugs!

An uncomfortable rug must be changed for one that is the correct size for the size and conformation of the horse.

While these measures will remove the cause of the horse's habit, he may have come to like doing it and may therefore continue it. He may be prevented from indulging in it by making him wear a bib, a hard, plastic object that is attached to the headcollar; it allows him to eat and drink, but prevents him from getting at anything under his mouth with his teeth. Once the cause of the rug-tearing has been removed and the bib has been worn for a period of time, perhaps two weeks, the horse may have been successfully weaned off the habit and the bib can gradually be left off, first in the day time and then at night. If however he resumes the habit when it is removed, he may always have to wear one whenever a rug is put on.

Some horses will still find a way of tearing their rugs, even with a bib fitted. Sometimes a horse will learn to rest the bib on his side, and will then gradually lower his mouth so that the bib slides up his side thus exposing the area behind his muzzle and enabling him to grab his rug with his teeth. When such a horse must wear rugs, the only alternative may be to fit a cradle, a neck frame made of wooden slats that prevents a horse from turning his head round to his sides at all. It is not a very pleasant thing for the horse to wear – but then paying out for rug repairs every week or so is not very pleasant for the owner!

Storing rugs

PROBLEM What is the best way to store rugs that are not going to be used for some time, in order to prevent mice damage and general deterioration?

SOLUTION It is very important that rugs to be stored are clean and thoroughly dry. An industrial washing machine such as may be found at many launderettes is ideal for the job, and the rugs should then be hung in a warm place to dry naturally.

Once dry, any leather attachments should be well oiled and smeared with grease, as should any buckles. A dry, warm day should be chosen to pack rugs away, so that no damp air is present. The rugs should be folded into a neat parcel and wrapped in newspaper, brown paper, or large paper bags. Plastic bags should not be used as these can cause condensation, dampness and ultimately rotting of the stitching and fabric. Old feed sacks are also to be avoided as the smell may attract mice.

Once parcelled up, the rugs should be put into a wooden trunk, an old suitcase or even an old chest of drawers that closes snugly: all these are likely to be vermin proof. They should then be placed off the floor, preferably indoors, or at least in a place that does not become damp.

TIP

Rugs should always be repaired before putting them away, as they may be needed in a hurry – there is nothing more annoying than not being able to use 'them because they must be sent away for repair.

Confidence crisis

SOLUTION The first and most obvious question to ask here is: 'Why?' A horse which used to load without a problem does not stop doing so for no reason. Usually the problem stems from fear or a lack of confidence. Although the owner may not be aware of it, it is highly likely that the horse has suffered a bad experience on one occasion, if not more. Alternatively he may have come to associate going in the box with something unpleasant – for instance, perhaps he doesn't like going to shows for some reason. First the owner needs to think hard to try and identify a possible cause. Did the horse knock himself in the box at any time? Was the box involved in an accident, even a minor one, while the horse was inside? Did the box have a different, perhaps less sympathetic driver? When at a show, did the horse have an unpleasant experience? Did he show a constant dislike of anything at a show, perhaps the loudspeakers or flags? Once a possible cause has been established, a programme of regaining the horse's confidence can be planned.

PROBLEM What can be done with a horse which used to be fine to load, but has steadily got worse to the point where he either refuses to enter the trailer or horsebox, or panics when he is in it?

TIPS

- When travelling the horse cannot anticipate corners, so accelerating and decelerating must be done gradually.
- Protective clothing should be worn during the training session as this in itself may be a cause of anxiety.
- Force should be avoided, as this will only serve to confirm a horse's anxiety.
- If possible, the horse should be unloaded somewhere safe and quiet in the countryside and just taken for a hack so that he does not always associate going in the horsebox with going to a show, or even a regular place.
- The horse should be constantly praised whenever he complies with his owner's wishes, but he should never be scolded. Simply withholding the praise when he does wrong will serve as a deterrent to bad behaviour, as long as praise at the appropriate time is plentiful.

First the horse should be coaxed into the horsebox, offered a reward, and then led out again. This can be repeated over a number of days so he learns that he is not necessarily going to be driven anywhere every time he enters the box. Once he seems settled and will stand quietly in the box, he can be offered his feed inside. He should be allowed to eat this, and can then be walked down the ramp and back to his normal routine. Next, the ramp should be closed while he is eating; then he may be let out and taken back to his normal routine again. Gradually such sessions can be developed until the horsebox is actually started and the horse taken out for a short ride with a sympathetic and careful driver; these rides may be made gradually longer, until one day the horse arrives at a show, or at the sort of occasion the owner feels may have caused the problem. He can be led around, and should generally just be allowed to take in all the sights and sounds. He can be offered a feed in the box, and then driven home. Gradually and with patient handling the horse should become confident again, but it may take some time.

Allowing a horse to stand and feed in the horsebox – without travelling – is a great way of helping him to relax by associating going into the box with something pleasant and normal

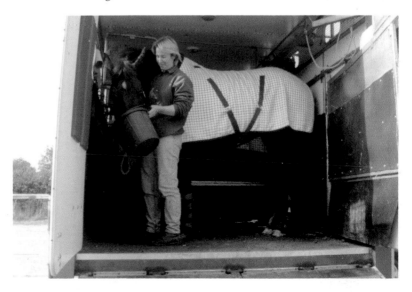

In a sweat

PROBLEM Some horses which are no trouble to box and which have an altogether placid temperament, nevertheless seem to travel badly, arriving at a show dripping with sweat and tucked up. Once they get off the box they seem to recover very quickly and appear none the worse for the experience until travelling home again. Why is this, and what can be done to prevent it? Could the horse be doped or have something put in his feed, or would he arrive at the show all 'doped up'?

SOLUTION First of all make sure that the cause is not physical – for instance heavy, warm rugs should not be put on a horse for travelling, nor those made from quilted, synthetic materials as these tend not to let the horse's skin breathe as he starts to warm up. During the summer months a summer sheet, and during the winter a light day rug are all that are needed for such a horse. During warm weather the humidity in a lorry can build up to quite a high degree, especially if there are several horses travelling in the lorry. All available windows should be opened, and air vents should be free from obstructions.

If there is no physical cause, the most likely reason for excessive sweating when travelling is stress. A number of factor can cause stress when travelling (see also page 39), however, those most likely to result in sweating are:

■ close confinement;
■ being next to an unfriendly horse;
■ nervous anticipation of the event at the end of the journey.

To rule out close confinement, the horse should be travelled in more spacious surroundings to see if he copes better and sweats less. Removing an unfriendly horse will obviously improve things if this is the problem. However, the horse should also be tried alone and with another more friendly companion, as solitude may prove a cause of stress in itself – he may prefer the company of even an unfriendly horse to being left alone. Nervous anticipation of an event is common and does take time and patience to remedy (see also page 41).

Sedating a horse is not the answer as this will interfere with his co-ordination and could cause him to stumble up the ramp, fall when in transit, or slip when being unloaded – all situations where injuries can occur. Calming herbs in the feed can be used, but these should be tried on a separate occasion before the horse is travelled to ensure that he does not have any adverse reaction to them.

As with many travelling problems, the solution lies in finding out what exactly it is that is troubling the horse, and taking the time to find a way of banishing his fear.

Dressed for warm-weather travel: a summer sheet

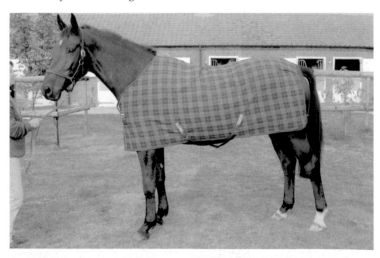

During the colder months a light day rug will provide a little extra warmth without overheating the horse should he begin to sweat

Horsebox horrors

SOLUTION

There are several reasons why a horse may travel better in a trailer than in a horsebox and usually the cause is a physical one:

- the horsebox may not be driven as sympathetically as the trailer and towing vehicle;
- the partitions in the horsebox may be too wide apart, so not providing the support the horse requires;
- the partitions may be too narrow, thus preventing the horse from establishing his footing;
- the leadrope may have been left too long, so allowing the horse to get his head around;
- there may be no bedding on the floor – even a non-slip floor benefits from some bedding, to soak up urine and prevent dung from making the floor slippery;
- the horse may prefer to travel forwards as he can in a trailer, rather than herringbone as is usual in a horsebox.

If there is access from the cab of the lorry to the horse's part, it is a good idea for someone to travel in the back with the horse so they can see how he is travelling; only then can the partition width or the length of the rope be assessed for the individual horse.

PROBLEM

Why is it that some horses travel better in trailers than in horseboxes, and what can be done to prevent a horse which travels badly in a horsebox from falling over and injuring himself?

TIP

If a horse does not 'plant' his feet when travelling – that is if he continually shuffles them about – he may have difficulty in distributing his weight when going round bends, up or down hill or over undulating terrain, and this can cause him to lose his footing and possibly to fall. To prevent this from happening, all the above measures should first be assessed to ensure the horse has optimum comfort when travelling. Occasionally other factors such as travelling alone, or excessive engine noise may be responsible for upsetting him. Protective clothing should be fitted to protect the horse in case of an accident – but the ultimate solution is to establish the cause of the horse's discomfort and to correct it quickly if he is not to lose confidence altogether and become a bad traveller.

Correct partitioning during transport is all-important if the horse is to travel safely and comfortably

Spoilt for choice

PROBLEM   Insurance is often a neglected aspect of horse management, either because it appears to be too expensive, or because people are all too ready to think 'It'll never happen to me'. What insurance options are available, and how can one be chosen that suits the needs and financial resources of the individual horse owner?

SOLUTION   Insurance to cover the unforeseen is a sensible, if not essential precaution to horse ownership. Riding and handling the horse with all due care and attention will help to cut down on injuries and mishaps, and similar precautions against intruders will help to prevent theft; but a horse and/or its belongings, both of which represent a great investment to most owners, can never be 100 per cent safe.

There are varying degrees of insurance cover: the basic option covers mortality from accident or illness, and loss by theft or straying may also be covered or may be an optional extra. Such standard policies are offered with varying degrees of risk, and the greater the risk involved the higher the cost of insurance; for instance the horse used for light hacking will be far cheaper to insure than one used for eventing. Most policies can be built up to suit individual requirements. For instance, the standard policy can then have optional cover added, including:

■   veterinary fees (see page 45);
■   personal accident (covering the owner or person authorised to ride/drive the horse in the event of an accident);
■   third party liability (in the event that a horse damages another person or his belongings);
■   immediate cover (see page 43);
■   loss of use (where a horse can no longer be used for the purpose intended).
■   saddlery and tack (see page 44);

If an owner's requirements do not fall into a standard category, a tailor-made policy may be arranged. Insurance can be paid for annually by cheque or credit card, or many firms now offer monthly direct debit payments; this allows payments to be spread throughout the year, although before commencing in this way it is sensible to check whether there will be any interest charges added to the full insurance cost.

Cover for personal accident is a serious consideration, especially for working owners

Excessive excess

SOLUTION An excess fee is the amount which has to be paid by the horse owner before the insurance company will pay out the remainder. This should be a fixed amount rather than a percentage. For instance, a fixed excess might be £100 of a veterinary fees' claim. However, some policies might state the excess as '£100 or 10 or perhaps 15 per cent of each claim, *whichever is the greater*'. Thus if the veterinary fees were £1,500, with the fixed fee a cost of £100 would have to be paid before the insurance company would pay out the balance of £1,400, but with the percentage the cost would be either £150 (10 per cent), or £225 (15 per cent)!

PROBLEM Before an insurance company will pay out, there is often an 'excess' fee to be covered. What is this?

Immediate cover

SOLUTION Some insurance policies do not commence cover for thirty days from the date it is taken out. This is of little use if a horse needs to be covered in a hurry. However, many insurers now offer immediate cover which can be arranged by paying with a credit card over the telephone. If it is likely that a horse is going to be purchased from an auction or sale, pre-warning the insurance company will help to expedite the matter. However, such immediate cover usually only covers a horse against accident, and full cover does not commence until the signed proposal document has been received by the insurer.

PROBLEM Sometimes it is not possible to arrange insurance cover so that it is in place for when it is needed. For example a horse might be bought at auction, or might need to travel unexpectedly, so how can it be covered under such circumstances?

If you plan to buy a horse at auction make sure that you can arrange cover from the fall of the hammer

Tack theft

PROBLEM Tack gets stolen or damaged quite often. Can tack be insured against theft and damage, and if so, what security arrangements might be expected by the insurance company?

SOLUTION Many equine insurance companies also cover tack, and often the policy that covers a horse will also cover its tack. Usually this is for theft, but damage cover can also be arranged. However, this must be checked as there may be certain conditions, the value of the tack being one, and where it is kept being another. Usually tack must be kept in a person's house, or in a locked building, secured with a mortice deadlock. If the tack is removed from these premises, perhaps in cases where the horse is taken to a show, it needs to be kept in a securely locked place when not in use. Should the tack be unusually valuable, a further fee may be requested.

TIP

Beware of insurance 'small print'. Providing it is clear what it contains, and that stipulations are complied with, there should be no problem when it comes to paying out. However, often the small print is not read properly, and claims are then rejected because these clauses have not been obeyed.

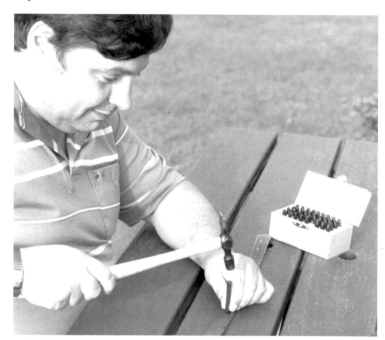

Marking tack with your postcode or other personal number will help with identification should it be recovered

Types of treatment

PROBLEM When a horse becomes ill, the last thing anyone wants to have to worry about is how much it will all cost. Can a horse be insured against veterinary fees, and if so, does such insurance cover all types of treatment?

SOLUTION Cover against veterinary fees is an optional choice over and above any basic cover. Usually such fees are covered up to a maximum price (at the time of writing [1997] a sensible figure for cover against accident and illness is about £2,000 per year), depending on the policy and the risk factor. Furthermore such insurance does not always cover all types of treatment. For instance, some policies do not cover alternative treatments such as physiotherapy, or hydrotherapy, so this should be clarified with the company before any premium is paid. Cover against veterinary fees should not be limited to a percentage of the sum insured, but should be that which is received per claim.

Vets' views

SOLUTION Most insurance companies do require a veterinary certificate, especially if:

- the horse is valuable; moreover the significance of value differs from one company to another, so this should be investigated at the outset;
- the horse has not been insured for over a year;
- the horse's insurance value is higher than its purchase price.

Horses of low value, brood mares and youngsters may be exempt from having to have a veterinary certificate. Moreover if the horse has suffered from an injury or illness in the past that is likely to recur, the insurance company may place an exclusion on the policy – this means they will not pay out for that particular condition, but that the horse is otherwise covered. Similarly if at the time of vetting the veterinary surgeon made a comment on the veterinary certificate about an existing injury or illness, the insuring company may put an exclusion on the policy to cover themselves against this. Once the horse has recovered, and providing a veterinary surgeon confirms that the horse is restored to full health and that the illness or injury is no more likely to recur in the horse in question than in any other horse, the exclusion can be lifted.

PROBLEM Before a horse can be insured does it require a veterinary certificate and if the horse is known to have had a health complication will this prevent it from being covered?

Most insurance companies do require the horse to be vetted before accepting your proposal

Part 2:
THE HORSE AT

GRASS

Social Behaviour
The herd hierarchy
Buddies
Bullies

Suitability for Living Out
The well-bred horse
Old-age pensioners

Maintaining Good Health
Field observations
Horse sense
Turning away
Limitations
Bringing up

Feeding
Hay there!
Meal-time mayhem

Rugs and Rugging
Rugging reminders
New Zealand or turnout?
Rug design
A sore point

Coping with the Weather
Fly frenzy
Snow

Management Problems
A new home
A stranger in the pack
Refusing to be caught
Extracting one horse from a group

Optimum Conditions in the Field
Fencing
Suitable shelters
Erecting a shelter
Field shelter design
Water worries
Maintaining a good pasture
Horse-sick land

Security
Peace of mind

The herd hierarchy

PROBLEM Is it safe to graze mares and geldings together in the same field, or are they best kept apart?

SOLUTION In a natural setting, herd life is matriarchal – that is, the leader of the herd is a mare, not a stallion, as is often thought. In the domesticated setting where geldings and mares graze together, a gelding is treated by the rest of the group as just another 'mare' so there are usually no problems grazing mares and geldings together, unless one of the geldings is a rig (shows stallion tendencies) and one or more of the mares is in season.

Horses have clearly defined rules within their field society, and as long as a young horse (mare or gelding) is allowed to associate with others, he will learn what is required of him. Horses live in this way because it is natural to their survival: a lone animal is at great risk from predators, whereas within a group there is a far higher degree of safety.

Obviously domesticated horses are not at risk from predators, but the instincts are still there, a group of horses in a domestic situation will still form a 'pecking order'. It will not necessarily be the oldest mare that heads the group, it can be an older gelding, but generally youngsters are more subservient. Left to their own devices horses will sort themselves out, and while there may be a few squabbles at first, horses rarely suffer great injuries – in fact, more harm can be done by keeping a horse away from his companions through fear of injury, because he can suffer great psychological stress.

Horses will naturally 'sort each other out' in the field, especially at feeding times, but usually they settle into their own 'pecking order' without too many problems

Buddies

SOLUTION Horses which are close companions are often 'split up' because their owners feel they cannot manage one while the other is around. However, this is simply a failure on the owner's part to teach the horse good manners and respect. If he isn't sure whether he can manage, and fears for his own safety he should take the process of separation and training gradually, especially with a young horse – but he must absolutely insist that the horse does as he is told. At first the horse can simply be walked around the paddock within sight and earshot of his companions, but *under the control of his owner*. This may progress to walking around a neighbouring field, and so to working away from his companions altogether. At no time should the horse be allowed to pull away from the owner, so adequate restraint in the form of a bridle and if necessary a Chifney bit should be used. Once a horse realises that he will be reunited with his friend after he has carried out any task required of him, he will generally work willingly. Trying to separate the horses when stabled will simply result in them fretting.

PROBLEM Horses can, and do, form close friendships with each other, usually with those of an equal standing in the 'herd'. However, this can prove difficult if one horse then frets and misbehaves if taken away from his friends. When stabling horses, should this field friendship be preserved by housing the horses next to each other, or should they be separated?

> **TIP**
>
> *The owner should always wear gloves and carry a schooling whip, which can be flicked with the left hand just behind the horse's shoulder to encourage him to move on if he is stubborn.*

Walk the horse around the paddock in sight and earshot of his companions, but make sure that you are in command at all times

Bullies

PROBLEM Why is it that some horses are really aggressive towards others, sometimes to the point of ostracising them from the field group, and how can a bully be prevented from hurting others?

SOLUTION While out in the field, each horse has his own 'personal space'. Family members and close friends will be allowed to enter this space, but others will not. It is quite natural for two horses that are not closely bonded to keep their distance from each other; it is not so much dislike, as merely not needing each other's company. However, some horses can take a real dislike to another individual, and then action must be taken if the horse is not to be bullied.

It is an owner's responsibility to ensure that his horse/s time at liberty is enjoyable and unthreatened, and this can only be achieved by ensuring that all the horses turned out together are congenial towards each other. Whilst it is in the nature of herd life that some horses are more dominant than others, unfortunately some are just plain bullies, and this results in the more subordinate ones being constantly driven away from the rest of the group, and generally deprived of their right to peace when grazing, drinking or dozing. It is bad management to allow such a situation to develop, and plain stupidity to allow it to continue. In fact there is very little that the owner can do, other than to remove one of the horses from the group, and it is the bully horse that needs to go, not the underling.

Sometimes it will satisfy the bully horse if the subordinate one moves away as he approaches, but if he actually goes for the other horse, then he must be removed immediately. Fortunately, horses are rarely vicious, but even so, a watchful eye must be kept on a group of horses grazing together to ensure that an acceptable pecking order has been achieved.

Some horses are really aggressive towards others, and a mere menacing look is enough to tell more subservient horses to keep away

---

TIP

Often a bully horse will cease his behaviour if put in a field with another horse which is more dominant than himself. A more dominant horse is not a more aggressive horse, simply one which has achieved a higher social standing within the group.

The well-bred horse

PROBLEM Can a finely bred horse thrive living out of doors, or is such a life-style going to result in health problems?

SOLUTION When considering whether a horse is a suitable candidate for outdoor living an assessment needs to be made of his proposed living conditions. The following list of requirements will help an owner to decide whether the facilities he can offer will provide everything his horse needs:

Food

Horses are trickle feeders, which means they require an almost constant supply of food in order to keep their digestive system working properly. Keeping a horse in a field obviously satisfies this need as long as there is an adequate supply of grass. However, the Thoroughbred, the Arab or any other such finely bred horse is unlikely to thrive at grass unless extra nutrition is provided: this should be in the form of concentrate feeds in relation to the horse's condition and workload, and hay when grass is in short supply.

Exercise

This is essential to the physical and mental health of all horses. While turned out the horse can exercise himself naturally, by moving around the paddock in order to graze, and by playing with his companions. The horse is an animal of a number of paces, all of which were designed to be employed; thus in order to maintain his physical health he must be able to extend his body and limbs and use them all. As the more finely bred horse is likely to be an active type, living out will be beneficial in this respect.

Company

Horses are gregarious animals, which means they like to live in the society of others. Quite apart from the survival instinct of there being safety in numbers, feral horses live in herds because they actually enjoy each other's company. Finely bred horses can become quite fractious if kept in solitude, so living out has another benefit in this respect.

Shelter

Every horse needs all-year-round shelter, but a finely bred horse will be particularly susceptible to the elements of sun, wind, rain and freezing temperatures. A natural weather-shield such as a band of trees or a thick hedge will not prove adequate in the winter, so a man-made field shelter will be required with a good deep bed. During harsh weather the horse may need proper stabling, and he will certainly have to be rugged up in warm, waterproof rugs.

By understanding these basic needs an owner can appreciate that the closer a horse is kept to a natural environment, the fewer problems will be created both for himself and his horse/s. Providing all the above points are considered and heeded, there is no reason why a finer bred horse should not thrive out of doors.

A well-bred horse can live out happily during the winter months providing it has adequate shelter, food and company

Old-age pensioners

PROBLEM   Do older horses suffer more from the effects of cold weather, and if they do, is it unfair to keep them out of doors during the winter months?

SOLUTION   Age is not a major consideration for the horse living outdoors, until he becomes very old. Older horses may be at slightly more risk from the effects of cold, wet weather and will probably need more food and rugs, but nevertheless being left to roam about freely does help to prevent them from becoming too stiff. Common sense should prevail, but as long as the horse is otherwise healthy and has all his basic needs provided, there is little need to stable him more as he gets older. A very old horse may be an exception, as his heating mechanism may not be quite what it should. However, in this situation you still need to weigh up the advantages and disadvantages: thus an old horse that has lived out all his life might start to fret if suddenly stabled, so a better solution might be to provide more rugs, food and shelter. The horse's own condition will be the crucial guide as to how well he is coping with living out: if he maintains his condition he is obviously coping well with the weather conditions, and the feed he is receiving is adequate; but if he starts to lose weight during cold weather this is an indication that he is losing too much body heat, and it will need correcting by the addition of rugs and more feed.

TIP

Rather than stable an older horse which is not coping so well with winter conditions, a better option may be to erect a shelter with a sliding bottom door that can be closed to keep the horse in when conditions are particularly harsh. This will help to prevent him fretting as he will still be in familiar surroundings.

A horse's condition is the crucial guide as to whether he is coping with living out of doors. This old mare looks poor and ribby, and would benefit from being well fed and stabled

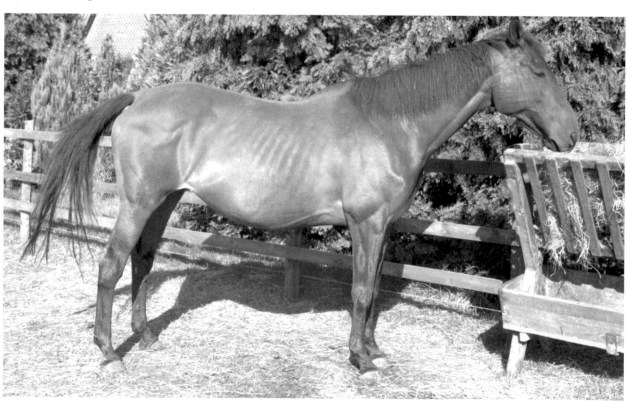

Field Observations

SOLUTION   The healthy horse should always appear bright and cheerful. Even though a particular horse may have his own individual idiosyncrasies, he should never appear 'sick or sorry'. Being alert is a good indicator of health, so an owner should check to make sure the horse is looking to see what is going on around him, or looks up when he or she approaches. Before going to catch the horse, the owner should assess how is he standing in the field: if he is standing dejectedly on his own, or shows any other unusual behaviour, then some sort of illness may be developing. The owner should always double check if unsure of his horse's state of health, by carrying out some physical tests (see page 54). If a horse usually whickers when he sees his owner approaching, they should take note if one day he does not. Potential problems should always be prepared for so they can be confronted and resolved in as short a time as possible. Although living outside is natural for the horse, it does not mean that he can look after himself: he is still dependent on his owner for his needs and this includes his health.

Observations which should be made when the horse is in the field include:

The way he is standing

The healthy horse will stand evenly on all four feet, or might rest a hind foot if he is feeling particularly relaxed.

The condition of his coat

Unless he is living out without a rug in the winter, a horse should have a nice glossy sheen to his coat. His natural oils will keep his skin and coat in good condition, even if he is not groomed every day. Flaky, scurfy skin may mean there is some underlying problem, so this should be investigated.

His appetite

Appetite is one of the first things to be affected if a horse is feeling off colour, so he should be observed to see if he is grazing normally. Unless a horse is known to be a fussy eater he should eat up well. Food left in a feed tub in the field should set an owner's warning bells ringing, unless perhaps the horse has had a recent change of environment – being turned out into a lush paddock when previously he was on a sparse one, for instance. Should a horse suddenly develop a poor appetite it is often a warning that colic or some sort of viral infection is to follow. If it is noticed that a horse frequently drops food from his mouth (known as quidding), he may have a problem with his teeth, so this needs immediate attention before his health starts to suffer as a result.

PROBLEM   When a horse is stabled, possible signs of illness can be picked up quite quickly and any departure from the normal pattern of drinking, eating and passing urine and droppings is easy to assess. When a horse lives out however, any early warning signs can readily go unnoticed. How can the horse owner ensure that he does not miss any signs of illness?

The healthy horse will be alert, and will show interest in his owner's approach

PHYSICAL EXAMINATION

When a horse is first visited in the morning, he should be checked over to make sure he has come through the night unscathed. To begin with, this will involve a simple look over to ensure he has no cuts, swellings or foreign objects embedded into his skin. Then a closer look should be taken:

■ His eyes should be bright and focused, and the eye membranes should be a nice salmon-pink colour. However, it is important to check these while a horse is in good health, as some horses have naturally paler membranes than others.

■ His nostrils should be moist with a nice salmon-pink colour inside. There should be no thick discharges although a few droplets of watery discharge can be quite normal.

■ His limbs should be free from heat or swelling.

■ His skin should be supple, easily passing back and forth on top of the underlying layers. It should feel warm and dry to the touch with his coat lying flat against his skin. If a fold of skin on the horse's neck is pinched it should immediately spring back into place once released (it is known as the 'pinch test'). If the pinch remains visible then the horse is showing signs of dehydration.

These are simple checks that should be carried out every day. If the results lead an owner to believe that all is well, he can leave his horse happily to graze. However, should he be at all worried, even if it is just a 'feeling' that something is wrong, then further investigations are needed and the horse should be brought into a stable and his temperature, pulse and respiration rates should be checked. Only when all this is done should a veterinary surgeon be called.

■ A horse's normal temperature is 100.5°F (37.9°C), although a variation up or down of about half a degree is normal. A vet should always be called if a horse's temperature rises above 101.5°F or falls below 100°F.

■ The normal pulse rate of a healthy horse at rest is in the region of 35 to 40 beats per minute. If this rate exceeds 50 at rest, then the cause requires further investigation.

■ While at rest a horse's respiration rate should be between 8 and 12 breaths per minute which should be even and regular (see also page 85).

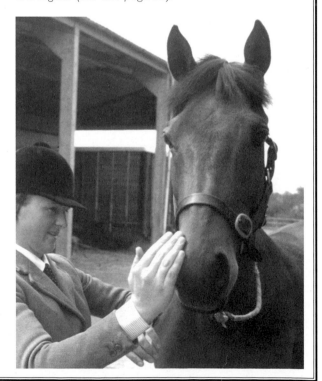

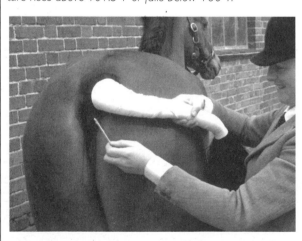

Horse sense

SOLUTION Horses do have a very good sense of taste in that they are able to detect what is palatable from the first bite, discarding anything less desirable from the mouth that has fooled the sense of smell. The four components recognised by the horse are sweet, sour, bitter and salt; his preference is usually for sweet or salty things, but others also have their appeal, and what may seem quite bitter to humans can have an acceptable taste to the horse. Many poisonous plants are bitter to the horse, and unless he is extremely hungry he will normally reject them. However, such plants can lose their bitterness when baled into hay, so an owner should always be on the lookout for this. Furthermore, a few horses do seem to acquire a taste for plants that are not good for them, even though other food is adequate. This may come from their natural instincts to 'dose' themselves in times of feeling ill with naturally growing herbs, or because their sense of taste is failing for some reason. Whatever the cause, the only way of preventing such poisoning is to ensure there are no poisonous plants in the horse's paddock. Removal should be complete, that is leaves, stem and roots.

PROBLEM If it is true that horses are able to distinguish between poisonous plants and edible ones, why do some suffer from ragwort, acorn and other forms of poisoning while grazing?

TIP

Acorns can prove a real problem where oak trees are in a paddock. Fencing them off is totally impractical as the spread of the branches is huge, and picking them up would take forever. Two methods of removal that work well are by rolling them into the ground after rainfall so that they are no longer accessible to the horse, or by sucking them all up with a paddock vacuum once a week during the acorn season; these vacuums can be hired.

A paddock vacuum is the ideal tool for clearing up acorns

Turning away

PROBLEM The term 'turning away' means letting the horse out into a paddock for a rest from work. If the horse has been in full-time work, does he require a period of 'letting down', or can he simply be turned out and left to his own devices?

SOLUTION Turning a horse away may involve him living out all the time, or being brought in to be fed or stabled overnight, depending on his breeding and for what work he is kept. Every horse that has competed regularly deserves a rest at the end of the season. While competing, he will have received constant attention and so he will need time to wind down, both physically and mentally. If he has been showing he will have been wearing a lot of rugs, so these will need to be removed gradually. It is both cruel and inviting illness if a pampered horse is simply thrust out to fend for himself; whatever has been taken away in the form of coat and body oils must be allowed to re-establish itself before the horse can be turned out all the time.

Only when an owner is sure he has hardened off his horse sufficiently well can he go out, but the right time, perhaps a sunny autumn day, will have to be chosen.

Before turning a horse away he should be allowed a period to 'harden off'. This clipped horse will obviously suffer as a result of being turned out without a rug in freezing weather

In comparison this horse (right) is certainly 'hardened off', and will live out without detriment to his health

---

TIP

Turning horses away also gives their feet a chance to recover from the rigours of shoeing. Once the shoes are removed the nail holes can then grow down and any little cracks will grow out. While turned away it is important that the horse is still checked and fed regularly.

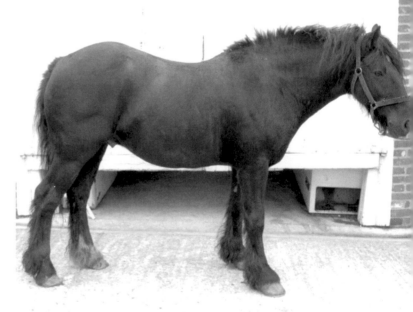

Limitations

PROBLEM Can a horse kept totally at grass still be worked hard and competed, or is this expecting too much of him?

SOLUTION It is often thought that a grass-kept horse will not have the same ability to perform as a stable-kept one. This is a mistake, however: it is undoubtedly more convenient to compete with the stable-kept horse as he is always on hand and usually clean when needed, but providing the grass-kept horse is well cared for, there will be no difference between his stamina and ability than that of his stabled companion. In fact it is often an advantage to compete the horse from the field because he will be quite relaxed and loose throughout his body, whereas a stabled horse may need more warming up before any real work can begin.

Obviously there are some drawbacks for the owner: for instance the horse cannot be ridden at any opportunity because he may be wet, or extremely muddy or both. Of course the horse could be brought in to dry him off first, but the owner may not have the time to do this. It may also be more difficult to keep a horse's coat in good order; other horses may chew it or bite his skin, which does not look too good for showing or dressage. However, there are few problems that cannot be overcome, and often a combined system works well for horses that are competing regularly: either they are kept in at nights and turned out during the day, or they are just kept in the day before a show.

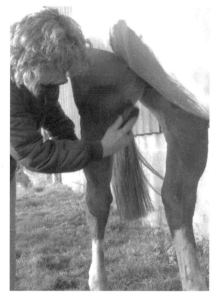

In wet, muddy conditions it can take some time to clean up a horse living at grass before a ride; it is essential to get saddle and bridle areas really free of mud to avoid chafing, and to have a thorough look all over the horse for cuts and bumps which may be concealed by a long, muddy coat

Bringing up

PROBLEM What does the term 'bringing a horse up' mean, and is there a correct procedure to follow when doing it?

SOLUTION 'Bringing up' is simply a term for putting the horse back into work after he has been turned away. Traditionally this means putting him back into a stable, although a horse can in fact be 'brought up' but still live out. After his holiday he should come up in good, sound condition and mentally refreshed, ready to start competing again. Bringing a horse up from grass involves the opposite sort of routine to turning away. Gradually the horse's workload is built up, as is his feed, and his general daily routine of grooming and strapping (see page 21) becomes more intense.

The right time to bring a horse up is, to a certain extent, a matter of personal choice and often depends upon individual circumstances. Some owners bring their horses up at the end of December in order to get an early start with youngsters and new prospects, while others may wait until mid to late January depending on what is planned for the year ahead. It is pointless for an owner to start work early in the year if they have little time to devote to their horse. In such a situation it is more beneficial to wait a few weeks until they know they can commit the time required to work the horse regularly.

TIP

When initially a horse resumes work, the first things to sort out are his coat and feeding programme. If his winter management and feeding regime have been well catered for, he should be in good health and carrying plenty of condition. This will ensure he stays in the best of health as work progresses.

Hay there!

PROBLEM   When feeding hay in the field it can become very wasteful if it is simply put onto the floor. What are the alternatives, and how can one greedy horse be prevented from hogging all the hay?

Hayracks with feed troughs under help to prevent wastage when feeding hay in the field. Mixing some cubes or coarse rations in with hay that has fallen into the trough can help to keep horses occupied for hours; they never seem to tire of sifting through for the last grain, and this is a good way of making them work for their food, as they would have to in their natural environment.

SOLUTION   Where there are several horses in the same field, feeding hay on the floor may be the only option as one pile more than the number of horses should always be provided; then even if an underling does get chased away from a pile there will always be another spare one to go to, and each horse can eat in peace.

Where there are only a few horses in a field, a hayrack is a better alternative. These are made of metal or wood; they are free-standing, and have a catch-tray underneath to prevent the hay from dropping on the floor and being trodden in. The round cage-type of rack used mainly for cattle should not be used for horses as they can get their heads stuck through the metal bars and then panic, and this could result in some nasty injuries.

Haynets are acceptable as long as they can be tied up high enough; often this will be to a tree or the side of a barn. The rope cords should always be checked for strength before leaving, and must be replaced at the first sign of fraying or weakness.

Meal-time mayhem

PROBLEM   Feeding more than one horse in a field can be fraught with problems, especially if an owner is not quick, efficient and careful. How can he ensure that all horses receive their fair share of food without endangering themselves in the process?

SOLUTION   The basic guidelines of feeding a group of horses safely and efficiently are:

- There should always be more tubs of food than horses, so that a more dominant horse cannot prevent an underling from eating.
- Short feed should never be tipped directly onto the floor. Either rubber field tubs, or mangers over the fence spaced at least 15ft (4.5m) apart from one another should be used.
- If there is one particularly dominant horse which makes feeding time difficult for the owner and other horses, he should be brought out of the field and fed alone.

- An owner should always try not to enter the field with feed buckets, as they can easily get kicked in the rush. Remove the tubs from the field, fill them with the feeds, then at feeding time simply push the tubs under the fence line. Move to a different part of the fence.
- Feed tubs should always be removed from the field once emptied.
- Feed tubs should be put inside tyres to prevent horses from tipping them over.
- If one horse is a particularly quick eater and is always trying to steal another horse's feed, he should have a large quantity of chaff added to his rations to slow him down.
- A constant supply of fresh water must always be available.
- Horses with special diets should be fed separately, either by being shut in the shelter or stable, or by being held on a lead rope outside the field (most horses will eat their feed within twenty minutes).
- A good alternative to concentrate feed for non-working grass-kept horses is a feed block. These are an excellent idea as they provide all the essential energy, protein, vitamins and minerals that the horse may need, with the added benefit that he can help himself as and when he likes.
- Haylage might be fed instead of concentrates to out-running horses; it is higher in nutrients than most hay, as a forage feed it is more natural to the horse's system than concentrate feeds, and is probably less wasteful. It may not be suitable for smaller ponies, however, because of its higher protein content.

A bucket is not ideal for feeding in the field, as they tip over easily; a feed tub in a tyre, or with a shallower design are more suitable

Feed blocks are a good alternative to concentrate feeds for non-working grass- kept horses

Rugging reminders

PROBLEM Do all horses need rugging during the winter months, or can a rug be more of a nuisance than a necessity to some horses?

SOLUTION When it comes to rugging horses that are kept out of doors there are two schools of thought. The first is that if a horse is allowed to grow his coat naturally, and if he is provided with shelter and adequate food, he does not need a rug. The second is that by rugging a horse both time and money can be saved, as the horse stays cleaner and warmer thus reducing the need for large amounts of food and hours spent grooming. Common sense must dictate whether an owner chooses to rug a horse or not. Obviously the finer horse will definitely need a rug, but a native or more common horse might be better off without one.

Over-protecting a horse can cause him to retain stores of fat, that in a more natural state he would use up in order to keep warm over the winter months. These fat reserves, in combination with a heavy coat, act as an insulating layer to reduce heat loss. While all horses need adequate shelter, many do not require rugs as their coats provide an excellent natural weather-shield. Furthermore, rugging a hardy type of horse or pony during the winter may predispose him to obesity the following spring

CAN A HORSE LIVING TOTALLY OUT AT GRASS BE BATHED?

A horse living at grass can be bathed during the summer months, but his owner must be sure that the overnight temperature is going to be warm for a few days afterwards; this will give the horse's coat time to re-establish its natural oils. A good brushing after bathing will also help the oils to establish themselves more quickly. Should the weather unexpectedly turn cold or wet in the following few days after this procedure the horse will need extra protection in the form of a waterproof paddock sheet. The mane and tail can be washed as and when required, without detriment.

New Zealand or turnout?

NEW ZEALAND RUG

These are designed to keep a horse warm and dry while he is turned out in the field. Most are made of waxed cotton or canvas, and need to be re-proofed once or twice within a season to ensure that no seepage occurs. The depth of a New Zealand rug is all-important, both for protection as well as to prevent it slipping. The sides of the rug should be long enough so that none of the horse's belly is visible; this will ensure that the rug is self-righting after the horse rolls, and will protect him in all weathers. Traditional New Zealand rugs have hindleg straps, and some have front-leg straps as well. The hind straps should be fitted so that they are not too tight (in which case they will rub when the horse moves) or too loose (the horse may risk putting his hooves through them when he lies down). One strap should be linked through the other, and adjusted until each strap is the width of a hand from the horse's leg. Having fastened the straps the horse should be viewed from the rear while walking away to ensure they allow free movement.

A TURNOUT RUG

This can mean a rug that is suitable for permanent wear, or it refers to a rug that is intended for a stabled horse only turned out for short periods. However, the latter is correctly known as a paddock rug, so specific usage should be checked before purchase. Turnout rugs are generally made of synthetic materials, and as with New Zealand rugs their purpose is to keep the horse warm and dry while out in the field. Modern turnout rugs tend not to have any leg straps but are shaped over the quarters and come with a tough fillet string and cross-surcingles to keep them in place. As long as the rug is deep enough, this design works extremely well, and it is especially good for horses which object to rear leg straps or have sores due to previously poorly adjusted ones. Modern turnout rugs also have the advantage over canvas or waxed materials in that they are lightweight, they come in degrees of warmth, and they tend not to rub the horse's shoulders. Turnout rugs designed for permanent use are completely waterproof, but at the same time allow moisture or perspiration to be transmitted to the outside of the rug. Therefore the horse can still maintain and regulate his body temperature as he would through his natural coat.

Seepage will eventually occur with any outdoor rug, but designs that have a seam running along the horse's backbone will yield more quickly than those with seams three-quarters of the way down each side – these are far better, as a degree of seepage here will cause very few problems. Traditional canvas materials need to be proofed in order to make them water-resistant; modern fabrics however, work on a hydrophilic proofing system whereby the horse's own body heat activates a molecular action that wicks moisture away from the horse's body, while the rug's outer shell remains water-resistant.

PROBLEM What is the difference between a New Zealand rug and a turnout rug, and is one better than the other for a horse that lives out permanently?

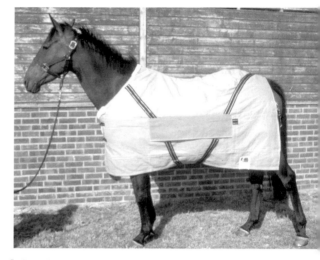

A traditional canvas-type New Zealand rug

The more popular 'turnout' rug

Rug design

PROBLEM   Are there any specific design points that should be considered when selecting a rug for permanent field use?

SOLUTION   The design of a rug is all-important as some are more suitable for certain types of horses than others. When a rug is being selected for field use the following points apply:

- It should be 'horse'-shaped. This may seem obvious, but it certainly is not to some manufacturers. Not so many years ago it used to seem inevitable that after a winter at grass the horse would come in with the hair rubbed completely off his shoulders. Nowadays a rug will have seams and gussets to provide a more tailored shape, especially behind the elbow, over the rump and around the neckline to offer more room for the points of the shoulders.

- It should not need a roller or surcingle. Most rugs now have either sewn on cross-over surcingles, or just hind, or hind and front leg straps. Where the rug does not have cross-over surcingles it needs to be deep so that it is self-righting after the horse rolls.

- The straps should be easily and fully adjustable, with no bulky buckles that may be uncomfortable for the horse when lying down.

- As well as being long enough from chest to tail, the rug also needs to be long enough from wither to tail. If these proportions are not right, the rug will not fit snugly.

- The rug should be deep enough in order to keep draughts away from the tummy. Extra deep rugs can be purchased, and these are a good choice for the wider type of horse. As a minimum guide a rug should come to at least just below the elbow and stifle.

A well-fitted rug will keep a horse warm and comfortable when out in the field

(Above) It is important that the front of the rug fits snugly around the shoulders, to prevent rubbing, but that it is still room enough to allow free movement

(Right) Hind leg straps should be snug so as to prevent the horse getting caught up in them when lying down or galloping around, but should not restrict the movement of the legs in any way

A sore point

SOLUTION   The areas most prone to rubbing and sores are the horse's shoulders, withers, and hips. Damage may be caused by the rug:

putting pressure on one or more of these parts;

slipping and therefore chafing vulnerable parts;

moving back and forth as the horse moves.

■   In all cases the cause is an ill-fitting rug, and the ideal solution is to change the rug for one that fits perfectly. If this is not possible, the shoulders, withers and/or hip points can be lined with sheepskin which will help to make the horse more comfortable – however, it will not alter the real cause. If sheepskin (or a similar fleecy lining) is used, it must be brushed regularly and kept clean. Some horses have the sort of shoulder conformation that appears to make them more vulnerable to rubbing whatever type of rug is used; in this case, an anti-rubbing vest will definitely help.

PROBLEM   Why do some rugs rub horses, and what can be done to prevent sores from occurring as a result?

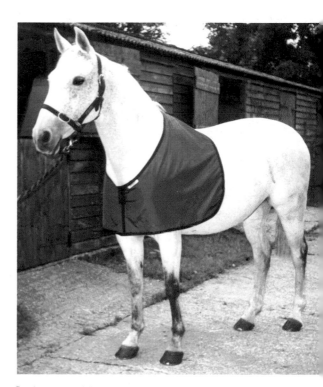

An anti-rubbing vest will help to prevent a horse vulnerable to rubbing from becoming sore; if rubbing has already started and you cannot change the rug, a vest may help the condition from getting any worse

This horse has clearly been rubbed – the ideal solution is to change the rug. Watch for early signs of rubbing, which often occurs on the shoulders or near the front buckle

Fly frenzy

PROBLEM   Flies and other insects can make a horse miserable in hot weather – no matter what he does to rid himself of these annoying little creatures, they follow him everywhere. What can an owner do to ensure his horse is not driven into a frenzy over the summer months?

A fly fringe correctly fitted

SOLUTION   A horse can become so irritated by flies that he will gallop around the paddock, as flies cannot keep up with him then – the problem is, the minute he stops they are back again. So as far as he is concerned, the choice is either to put up with the irritation, or to gallop until he is exhausted – that is, unless his owner intervenes as he should. Flies should never be discounted as simply being natural pests that the horse should learn to cope with: they are in fact a very real threat to the horse's health and their effect should never be underestimated. They can cause infected sores from bites, or they can irritate the eyes to such an extent that they become sore and inflamed. To reduce the effect of flies an owner should:

- Ensure a shelter is available (see page 74), as flies do not like to follow a horse into a cool, dark place.
- Provide the horse with a fly screen, fringe or mesh hood; the latter are very good because they do provide total protection of the head. They are fairly large to allow for movement, but they should fit close to the skin to prevent flies entering the hood and then driving the horse mad with their furious buzzing as they try to escape.
- Use an *effective* fly repellent. Many of the preparations that can now be bought over the counter only last for a short period of time. Ask your veterinary surgeon about residual repellents, as these can successfully last for days, rather than hours.
- Add garlic to the horse's food, because the smell acts as a fly deterrent.

Snow

PROBLEM   What effect does snow have on horses, and are there any illnesses that can occur as a result of the horse living out in snow?

SOLUTION   Horses can do very well out in the snow without any interference from their owners. In fact, owners can often do more harm than good by over-compensating for what *they* feel to be unacceptably cold weather. A non-Thoroughbred horse's winter coat is perfectly capable of keeping him warm underneath. It is not uncommon to see a horse with inches of unmelted snow on his back, which just goes to prove what a good insulator his coat really is. In fact, more important than protecting the horse from the cold in such conditions, is to protect him from the *wind*.

When snow is lying on the ground, owners should be vigilant because the horse's feet and legs will be more prone to certain ailments. As the snow keeps the lower legs constantly wet they are more susceptible to abrasions, and then of course mud fever is a real threat. In addition, owners should be aware that the horse's feet are not designed to cope well in snow; they are concave in shape, and as a result the snow packs into them, thus forming four 'ice' shoes which can be very uncomfortable for the horse. In such conditions the feet need to be picked out regularly; applying a layer of Vaseline or grease to the soles of the feet may help to prevent the snow from collecting and packing into them.

Another consideration during snow is the field boundaries. Ditches can often fill up, leaving no evidence of where they are, and lakes or ponds can freeze over; should a horse fall into either the consequences may be horrific – and such things do happen, as the fire brigade will confirm. If these particular features are in a field, owners need to be extra careful, and an emergency building must always be available so a horse can be brought in should the weather conditions become too tough.

There is no need to worry about your 'outdoor' horse in snowy conditions: providing he is well fed and checked regularly he will be perfectly happy. In fact horses often seem to really enjoy the snow!

A new home

PROBLEM

Does moving a horse to a new home have any effect on him and if it does how can the horse's owner help him to settle into his new environment quickly?

When moving a horse to a new field, check to make sure there are no hidden dangers lurking in long undergrowth

SOLUTION

Having just brought a new horse home, or when moving from one livery yard to another, an owner will have to allow his horse a period of acclimatisation, so that he may adjust to his new surroundings. First he should be allowed to explore his new paddock without the threat of any other more dominant horses. He might not like to be completely on his own, so the provision of an old pony or a more docile horse for company may have a calming effect. At first he is likely to gallop around, generally getting a feel of the space. Then he will take a closer look into all the corners; and lastly he will sniff the boundaries, locate the water trough and then graze. All of this may take a few minutes or a few hours – but it will be days before he really settles, so the owner must keep a watchful eye on him.

Before any horse is turned out into an unknown paddock, some field checks need to be carried out to ensure his safety:

- There should be no hidden hazards such as chain harrows, or rollers lying discarded in long grass by a farmer.
- There should be no litter. Broken bottles and food wrappings can often stray into paddocks, or be left by 'picnickers' if the field has a right of way.
- The fencing should be safe and secure.
- The watering facilities must be clean and suitable.
- There should be no poisonous plants growing, and if there are these must be removed, leaves, stem and roots.

If the field is the owner's property, these checks will seem obvious, but no owner should assume that they will automatically have been carried out at a livery yard. Most places are vigilant and *do* carry out regular checks, but unfortunately some yards just don't know any better, or simply do not care. It is not so rare to see horses grazing in fields full of ragwort, barbed wire or other such hazards; and every owner should ensure that his horse is not one of them.

TIP

It is hard to imagine how a horse feels about changing homes, and an owner can never really know how affected his horse is by a move. The best an owner can do is to try and understand how the horse feels, and to allow for any odd behaviour over the first few weeks. He might find it helpful to imagine that someone has sold his house without him knowing about it. He is then put in a car, taken on an unknown journey and dumped in another house. Obviously he will feel strange and probably very angry at first. However, gradually he will come to know where everything is, and will eventually claim the new home as his own. It does not happen quickly and there will be times when he still yearns to be back in his old home. Given our knowledge of a horse's memory, there is no reason to suspect that horses do not have the same yearnings.

A stranger in the pack

SOLUTION Unless a horse portrays a particularly dominant nature then he is likely to be shunned if he is simply turned out into a paddock to fend for himself with horses that are well established as a group. Where a whole *group* of horses is turned out at the same time into a new paddock they usually settle well after an initial inquisitive period; because none of them will have yet claimed the land as his own, each can find his own space and settle into his accepted place. It is when a new horse is introduced to an already established group that problems can occur, so introductions should be gradual. The ideal way of doing this is to proceed as follows:

- The horse should be turned out into a paddock adjacent to the one that contains the other horses. Ideally there will be a walk-way between the two paddocks, so that the horses cannot actually touch each other over the fence, but they can get used to seeing and smelling each other.
- After a day or so, one of the horses from the established group (ideally one of middle rank) is turned out with the new horse.
- After another day the rest of the group can be taken from their field and put in with the pair, or the pair can be put in with the established group.

There may be some initial squabbles, but this method usually causes few real disputes as the new horse has been gradually acquainted with the others.

PROBLEM No owner wants to turn his horse out into a group of others only to see him kicked, bitten and generally shunned. How can a new horse be introduced to a group without him getting hurt or being outcast?

These two horses quite happy in each other's company, but this relationship probably took some time to become established

After a couple of days grazing in an adjacent field, one member of an existing pack can be put out with the new horse to help establish a companionship between the two, before introducing the other horses

Refusing to be caught

PROBLEM Allowing himself to be caught by a human is something that a horse should learn correctly as a foal. If this most important lesson is not taught at this young age it can set the scene for a long and frustrating battle. How can a horse that refuses to come to his owner be caught and how can such a horse be taught to accept, once and for all, that he must come when required?

SOLUTION There is no better teacher than a foal's dam, so everyone who breeds a foal should take advantage of his unique position and teach it to be caught without a fuss. Thus whenever the mare is caught, the foal should also be rewarded for coming with her. Rarely does a foal taught in this way pose future problems.

The older horse should always be approached quietly and calmly, and should be informed of his owner's presence – the owner should talk soothingly to him as he draws close. A horse cannot see someone approaching from behind until the last minute and so he should always be approached towards his head and from the side, this will prevent him from becoming too startled. Such an approach will also ensure that the horse cannot kick out or barge his owner.

Where a young horse has not been taught properly to accept being caught, it may be necessary to make a three-sided pen with a slip rail to the back, in one corner of the field. Often the only way to catch such a horse is to herd it into the pen and have someone slip the rail across, and in order to gain his trust he can be fed in the pen, and then let out again. Once this has been accomplished a few times he will soon come to the pen of his own accord, whereupon he can be handled and generally taught some manners.

There are times when even the most obedient of horses will not be caught – perhaps they have recently been turned out onto a lush pasture and would rather not come back in! Generally, however, it is

A catching pen

the older horse that refuses to be caught on a regular basis which proves most problematic.

Refusing to be caught is a disobedience. While staying out grazing might be a more attractive option, the horse should have learnt to respect the wishes of his owner. There are a few methods that can be employed to teach him that when he is called he is expected to come. What owners must not do – and everyone feels like it at times – is to throw the headcollar at the horse as he disappears down the field showing a clean pair of heels!

What method is employed will depend on whether there are other horses in the field or not. If there are not, the horse can be trained to come for food. At first a bucket with some nuts in it will be needed, which is rattled quite loudly; the owner stands at the gate and encourages the horse to come by shaking the nuts and calling his name. If he does approach, a few nuts can be put into the hand and the rest should be deposited on the other side of the fence. If the horse comes for the nuts, he should be given them while the headcollar is swiftly put on. He must be generously praised for coming, and once on the other side of the gate he can be offered the rest of the nuts. Most horses quickly learn to come if they know they will be rewarded for doing so. In time the bucket can be dispensed with as just a few nuts or a carrot in the hand will be sufficient to reward the horse. An owner should always remember to call his horse as well, as this encourages him to come to the voice, which can be very handy if on occasion the reward is forgotten.

Other horses can be bluffed into being caught if they will not come for food. If the horse is the sort that allows his owner to get quite close, then runs off when he is just a few feet away, he is 'trying him out'. First, the owner should put the headcollar around his neck, so that his hands are free. Then he should stride positively down the field, walking straight past the horse; he should stop when some way past him, but should not turn around. By this time the horse is sure to be looking at his owner, but the owner must not look back at him. Instead, he should walk a few paces backwards and stop again. The idea is not to make the horse feel threatened but to incite his curiosity. One out of two horses will take a few steps towards their owner and then hesitate. At this stage the owner should walk forwards, *away* from his horse a pace or two. It can be amazing, but many horses will take a few paces towards their owner of their own accord. Still the owner does not look at his horse, but makes out that he is looking at something on the ground. Eventually the horse's curiosity will either get the better of him, or he will lose interest. It has been known for horses which are notoriously difficult to catch, to almost try to stick their head in the headcollar themselves, when employing this method. Others do not respond at all unfortunately and will still run off at the very sight of their owner entering their field.

Chasing the horse around the field until he is tired out will do no more than get the owner fit, and he will undoubtedly tire before the horse does. However, the horse's herd instinct can be harnessed: thus coming up from behind him will drive him on, while coming from the

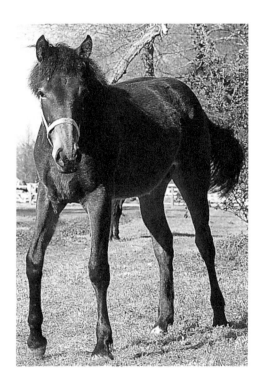

Once a horse has approached of his own will he can be offered a titbit as a reward

BEING CRUEL TO BE KIND

Should a horse be such a difficult character that no matter what is done he still refuses to be caught, then he must be punished. The best way of doing this is simply to withhold his feed – an owner should not waste his time chasing him around the field, nor should he relent and leave his feed out in the field for him. Sooner or later (usually after he has gone hungry for the night) the horse will behave himself and accept being caught without fuss.

Once a horse learns to associate being caught with something pleasant, and refusing to be caught or misbehaving with something unpleasant, he will rarely cause problems when trying to catch him. The process can be a lengthy and extremely frustrating one, but usually once the deadlock is broken the problem is solved.

Horses are naturally inquisitive and you can play on this when trying to persuade an awkward horse to be caught

front will cause him to back off. Going out into the field mob-handed might result in catching the horse, but it will not teach him anything, except to try harder to get away from his assailants the next time. It is important therefore that a horse learns to come because he knows it is what is expected of him. Some horses will get bored if the owner walks after them a few times, and will suddenly turn round and allow themselves to be caught. Such a horse should always be praised and rewarded for doing so.

If a horse is turned out with a few companions, one or more of the obedient horses can be offered a few nuts – although a bucket of nuts must *not* be taken into a field of horses or the owner is in danger of being mobbed. Horses have a natural inquisitiveness, so if the one who will not be caught is ignored while others are fed he may be tricked into being caught.

In the long term, patience is the key: the aim is to teach your horse that if he allows himself to be caught whenever his owner wishes, the result will always be pleasant – a treat or reward of some kind. While such lessons are being taught to the horse he should wear a field-safe headcollar with an 18in (45cm) length of breakable twine attached to it, doubled up to form a 9in (23cm) loop; as the horse takes the food from the owner's hand, the leadrope is attached to the loop of twine. This prevents you snatching at the headcollar in an effort to secure the horse, a practice which upsets many horses. Once caught, the horse should be brought in and fed; he should not be ridden or have anything done that he finds unpleasant, such as bathing him for instance. His time in should be totally enjoyable so that he begins to look forward to coming in.

Extracting one horse from a group

SOLUTION In order to make such an operation as smooth as possible, all horses should be taught to turn swiftly on their forehand when led. Once caught, the horse should be led quickly to the gate, which should then be unlatched, but held firmly with the hand that is not holding the leadrope. Any horses gathering around the gate should be encouraged to move behind the led horse, and thus behind the gate once opened. Once this has been accomplished, in one swift movement the gate should be pushed open, the led horse directed to walk through the opening but with his head still held, so that directly he is through the gate he must turn on his forehand in order to face the latch. The second his hind legs are through the gate, it can be quickly pulled shut, denying other horses the opportunity of barging through. The whole process needs to be very swift, but it is undoubtedly the most effective way of extracting one horse from a group, and is quite easy to accomplish with a horse that has been taught obedience.

Where many strange horses are passing in and out of a yard, a catching pen will provide a fail-safe system of preventing loose horses from escaping while one is brought in. This is simply a pen of about 12ft (3.6m) square with a gate at either end: one leads into the field, the other allows access beyond the field. Once a horse is in the pen and the field gate is closed behind him, there is no way others can barge past or kick, which obviously greatly reduces any danger. (See also page 68, Refusing to be caught.)

PROBLEM Removing one horse from a field where there are several others turned out can be tricky, especially when the horse's companions also want to come in. How can a horse be bought through the gate without being barged or kicked in the mêlée, and how can the others be prevented from escaping?

Teach your horse to turn on his forehand quickly when being led through the gateway, away from a group of other horses; this is something you can practise with your horse on your own, in less pressurised conditions

Fencing

PROBLEM   What sort of fencing can be used for horses, and are certain types more suitable than others?

SOLUTION   Various types of fencing are used to enclose horse paddocks, some more suitable than others, but whatever is used it must meet certain criteria. Obviously it needs to be high enough that the horse will not be able to jump out; however, the bottom rail or strand should not be so low that he could trap his hoof between it and the ground. It should be strong enough to prevent him from pushing it down or snapping it, and it must be clearly visible so that he doesn't run into it. Any sharp corners should be fenced across to prevent him from becoming trapped or wedged.

Natural hedges make an excellent field boundary as long as they do not become so sparse in winter that a horse can push through and escape. They are easy to maintain, and avoid the cuts and injuries that can occur from accidents involving fences. If the hedge is still establishing itself, it is a sensible safety measure to put secure fencing in front of it, so that the horse cannot simply push through.

Ditches are not a particularly safe form of enclosure: they need to be deep and wide enough to deter a horse from jumping over them, but if chased, a horse could fall in and then be unable to get out.

Post and rail is strong, clearly visible and safe. Two or three rails can be used depend-

(Above) Barbed wire fencing should never be used for horses

(Right) Clearly visible, wide-tape, electric fencing; not as nice to look at as post and rail, but very effective, and much cheaper to erect

ing on whether ponies or larger horses are kept. To ensure stability and strength there should not be more than a 6ft (1.8m) span between posts, and these should be 5in by 3in (13 by 8cm), and dug about 2ft (60cm) into the ground. The posts should be back-filled so that they will 'give' in an emergency and not snap under pressure. To protect them from winter weather they should be treated with creosote in late summer.

Stud rails can be used as an alternative to traditional wooden rails. They are made of high tensile wire covered with a wide plastic band, and are therefore clearly visible and strong. They are a good choice as they need very little maintenance and are completely safe.

Wire fencing, whether plain or barbed, cannot be recommended for horses. While barbed wire is the most problematic, any type of wire can cause horrific injuries. When it is first put up it is taut, but it soon sags and horses have little respect for it, so putting their head and legs through it at any opportunity. It is always best avoided.

Electric fencing this is available in two varieties – the sheep-netting sort is not at all suitable for horses; however, the type manufactured specifically for horse paddocks is excellent. It comes in wide white bands so is clearly visible, and is ideal for sectioning off fields to provide a rotation system.

Stock netting should never be used; not only does this example have a strand of barbed wire along the top, there is also always the danger of a horse getting a leg caught in the wire

Post and rail fencing is excellent for horses. The tops of the posts should not extend above the top rail, and the posts should be on the outside

(Left) Metal hurdles are strong, durable and relatively maintenance free, but make sure you regularly check that it is secure

Suitable shelters

PROBLEM Providing satisfactory shelter seems to be one of the most disregarded aspects of caring for a horse at grass. Are natural forms of shelter such as hedges or trees sufficient, or does the horse really need a purpose-built shelter?

SOLUTION Natural shelter is usually at best a densely leafed band of trees, but in pouring, driving rain the horse must still feel cold and miserable. In addition, during the winter months such natural shelter generally becomes sparse and inadequate.

A purpose-built shelter affords a much greater degree of warmth and comfort should the horse wish to take advantage of it; he can get out of draughts and keep himself completely dry, and it certainly provides a more comfortable option even if it is not essential to his well-being.

Field shelter design

SOLUTION
When putting a man-made shelter into a field, some thought should be given to the purpose for which it is to be put:
- will it be used more in summer than winter (perhaps because the horse/s are stabled at such times);
- is it required for only one horse, or several?

Where there are several horses in a field, the ideal is more than one shelter, although this can be costly and may take up more room than is really available. If it is only possible to provide one, then this must

PROBLEM
Can an owner construct a field shelter himself for his horse/s or should only purpose-made ones be used, and why would one design be chosen over another?

It is not necessary to lay a concrete base for a field shelter since it is not exposed to the same volume of urine as a stable. A nice thick bed is all that is really required, because as long as the shelter is not sited so that rain will run into it, it should stay nice and dry. The horse can be allowed to eat the grass inside a newly erected shelter for the first few days, before a bed is put down.

A well-made field shelter

The doorway to a field shelter should be high and wide enough to allow a horse easy access. Where two or more horses are sharing the same shelter it is preferable to have an entrance and an exit opening, so that no horse can become trapped inside by a more dominant one. In this respect a more sensible design would be a semi-circular shelter, because any horse which felt threatened could then easily make his escape; this idea does not seem to be popular, however. Alternatively the lee side of the shelter could be left open.

be large enough to accommodate all the horses in the field. Shelters come in many forms, some of which the owner may be able to construct safely himself – the simplest is a wall of straw bales supported by a wooden framework with a waterproof covering and a roof made of corrugated iron, although obviously this can be only a temporary measure and must be thoroughly secured. A large shed is preferable and this can be bought or constructed from surplus wood. Another way of acquiring a field shelter is through the classified advertisements in newspapers, where second-hand ones may be advertised. Occasionally they can be seen for sale at farm sales for little cost. If the stable yard butts up to the edge of the field the end stable can be utilised by making an opening in the side to allow the horses easy access. There are many firms manufacturing field shelters and generally they are very good designs. However, many owners do find the cost prohibitive.

Erecting a shelter

PROBLEM
Can a field shelter be erected anywhere in a paddock, or does some thought need to be given as to its site?

SOLUTION
A field shelter should be erected so that the back of it will take the brunt of the prevailing wind; this is usually so that the front faces the south. It should be sited either very close to the fence line so that a horse cannot get behind it, or far enough away from it so that there is easy access behind it. It should not be put in a corner of a field as this allows a bully horse to trap another up against it, nor under overhanging branches as these may annoy or scare the horse by constantly rubbing back and forth on the roof, perhaps spooking him and preventing him from entering the shelter altogether. Fallen, rotting leaves also make a mess of the roof. Some thought should also be given to the approach, in that it should be easy to push a barrow in and out in order to muck it out, and take in fresh supplies of hay.

Although not always possible, as many of the following requirements as is practical should be observed when siting a shelter:

- It should be sited on the highest part of the field, as this will prevent rain from running into the bottom of it, or the floor inside from becoming too wet.
- The back should face north or east.
- There should be easy access behind, or none at all.
- The shelter should be safe: no nails or other projection sticking out, no low beams or broken windows.
- The entrance should be as high and as wide as possible to encourage horses to enter, and to provide an easy escape if necessary; a completely open side is probably best.
- The structure must be strong enough to withstand horses rubbing or kicking the sides.
- A single pitch roof is fine but obviously this will need to slope backwards.

Water worries

SOLUTION Self-filling, galvanised water troughs are ideal for horses, although they can be costly to install. Alternatively an old bath tub that has had its taps removed can be employed safely at a fraction of the cost; it should be panelled upwards from the bottom to prevent a horse from trapping his feet underneath, but otherwise it is quite adequate. Obviously it will need to be cleaned out regularly, but because all you need do is simply pull the plug out, this is not a problem. It will help if this kind of trough is sited near to a water supply, so that filling and cleaning can be carried out with minimal effort.

Natural water supplies are provided by streams and rivers. However, it is important that the approach is firm and gradual, and the bottom should be gravel, not sand. Also the water must be running, otherwise it will become stagnant. A stream that has steep or crumbling banks should be fenced off to prevent use, and an alternative supply provided. To help prevent water buckets from freezing inside a shelter during cold weather they should be lagged. To do this, place a bucket onto a polystyrene sheet inside a thick, tough plastic bag, or hessian sack. Then fill the space between the bucket and the outside wrapping with hay to form an insulating cavity. Tie the outer covering securely around the bucket, and tuck in any loose ends. Then put the whole thing is inside an old tyre to prevent it from being tipped over. It can then be filled up.

Water troughs should be checked twice daily during freezing weather. This is so important that it cannot be stressed enough. It may surprise some owners that one of the main causes of colic in grass-kept horses in cold weather results from dehydration brought on by a lack of water. If an owner has a horse kept out of doors during freezing weather he must break and remove the ice on his trough *at least twice daily*. This is an owner's *duty*, and if he fails to do this, it constitutes a clear case of neglect. It can help to put a heavy football into the trough, as this will move in any breeze and so keep a small area free from ice, thus allowing the horse some access to the water below. A clever horse will learn to push on the ball in order to obtain water, in the same way that horses will learn to use an automatic drinking bowl; however, this should not be relied upon as a means of the horse getting enough water for himself.

PROBLEM Water is the most vital ingredient to a horse's health and well-being. It must be fresh, and available at all times in a suitable, safe container. What is the safest type of water trough to use in the field; can natural water supplies be utilised; and how can water supplies be prevented from freezing over during sub-zero temperatures?

A natural yet potentially hazardous water source, safely fenced off with electric tape

Placing a ball in the water trough can help to stop the top layer totally freezing over

Maintaining a good pasture

PROBLEM   What can be done to 'refresh' a paddock after horses have been grazing it for some time?

SOLUTION   Chain harrowing will help to stimulate a paddock, particularly if it has been over-grazed. It is best done twice a year in spring and autumn, in order to aerate the soil and so allow it to refresh itself. The prongs on the harrows will also gather dead grass, which is detrimental to any new grass trying to get through, and the process will also disperse piles of dung which would otherwise discourage the horse from grazing those areas. Horses avoid soiled grass when grazing.

Chain harrowing a paddock helps to aerate the soil

If harrowing is carried out purely to spread piles of manure, it is best done when the weather is very hot; the worms present will then be exposed to hot, dry conditions under which they cannot survive. Harrowing during moist, warm conditions simply allows the worms a greater run of the field as they are carried over its entire site and can live quite nicely under clumps of warm, moist dung.

Rolling a paddock is an efficient means of flattening unwanted lumps and bumps. Where a field has been poached, it will dry into very hard ruts within a few days of hot weather, so the time to roll is when the soil is still soft and springy. A very heavy land roller pulled behind a tractor is needed for this job, so that the land is levelled nice and evenly.

Horse-sick land

PROBLEM   What can be done to improve the quality of land that has been overgrazed by horses?

SOLUTION   The very first thing to do is to remove all the horses from the land. Secondly, the field will need to be fertilised, and then rested to allow for regrowth. Most paddocks need fertilising – or 'top dressing' as it is often known – on a regular basis, in order to put back what the horses are constantly taking out of the soil. However, it is important to discover the fertility status of the land before deciding what to treat it with; obviously it would be pointless and wasteful to provide something that is already in abundance. Initially the pH value of the soil needs testing, because if this is not at its optimum the fertiliser used may not be totally effective. Acid soils are particularly troublesome as they are a haven for weeds, to the point where the weeds take over and the grass begins to perish. Soil testing can be carried out by a local agricultural advisory service, and this is advisable if there is a particular problem. However, soil-testing kits can also be bought from local garden centres, and these are simple to use and give satisfactory results.

The normal pH value for soil is 6.5, although anywhere between 6 and 7 is acceptable: the more acid the soil, the lower the pH reading. In order to rectify acidic soil, lime needs to be added to the paddock. The recommendations on the bag should be followed carefully, and reassessed until a satisfactory pH level reading is achieved. An annual reassessment should then be carried out, adding lime when necessary to bring the pH level up to its optimum.

Having adjusted the pH to a correct level, an appropriate fertiliser may be considered. The aim is to provide palatable forage of good nutritional quality, and in order to do so, the main nutrients such as potash, nitrogen and phosphate need to be in good balance, with the secondary nutrients which include sulphur and magnesium, and also the trace elements; so there is a lot to cover! However, many manufacturers now produce specially prepared formulas which provide the correct nutrient levels in the right balance, and which are flexible enough to satisfy the needs of most pasture requirements. 'Force feeding' the grass by using high levels of quick-acting nitrates is not advisable; these will provide quick growth, but not the *quality* of growth that is needed. The type of fertiliser used will also depend upon whether the grass is required for hay or grazing. Every manufacturer's recommendations are slightly different, so an owner can only be guided by the information supplied with the particular brand used. Obviously horses must be removed from the paddocks to be treated, until the treatment has had time to take effect. This may be anything between seven and forty-two days, but certainly not before the granules have been thoroughly washed in.

A paddock that has been overgrazed by horses needs immediate weed treatment, all dung removed, top dressing and at least six weeks' rest before horses can beneficially graze the land again

Dressing a field at exactly the right time can be a matter of luck as well as judgement. The fertiliser needs to go on before any new spring grass starts to come through, and within 48 hours of rainfall. If the timing has been wrongly judged and no rain falls, the soil should be lightly harrowed again so that the granules are thrust to soil level, where moisture from dew will help to disperse them.

It is important to look after your land properly all year round. Fertilising a paddock needs to be done at the right time for maximum benefit to new growth

Peace of mind

PROBLEM
Every owner's nightmare is that one day he will go to the paddock to find his horse missing. What can an owner do to protect his horse from being stolen, or to try and ensure recovery if he is?

SOLUTION
It is up to the individual owner to provide maximum security for his horse. All horses turned out into fields need protection, especially if they live out all the time. Thieves will have observed that they live out, and will wait until the time is right to pounce.

Sometimes a deterrent is all that is needed. First, the field gate should be padlocked at both ends (with current BSI locks); there is little use just padlocking one end, as a gate can always be just lifted off its hinges by someone determined to gain access. Heavy duty chains will certainly make a thief think twice if he was intending to cut the metal, so these should be used wherever possible.

There are alarms available on the market that are triggered by the action of the gate opening – although someone must be within earshot, and preferably sight of the field. It is inadvisable to keep a horse in an isolated field away from an owner's home as these remotely placed horses are easy prey for the discerning thief. An owner should also be aware that horses are not only taken at night-time, so the alarm and locks should always be on whenever horses are in the field.

Electric fencing may provide a deterrent to opportunist thieves, if they unexpectedly get a shock. However, it is not a fail-safe system as professional thieves will come prepared with rubber gloves and wire cutters. If the gate leads out onto a road, it should be re-sited if possible to where it is in view of some houses or the yard.

It is also a good idea for owners to visit their horse as early in the morning and as

A gate padlocked at both ends will help to deter would-be thieves

late at night as is possible. They should try to ensure that there is no set routine or pattern, so anyone 'casing' the area for a suitable horse can see them arriving at different times; and they should particularly look out for any dubious-looking people, especially if these stop outside the field on more than one occasion. Any suspicious behaviour should be reported to the police, along with relevant descriptions and number plates. A crime prevention officer can be contacted through the local police station, and he will be pleased to offer advice on securing premises, and on local crime prevention schemes.

Security lighting will also deter thieves, or may well cause them to fail in any attempt to steal a horse. A passive infra-red detector will be invisible to the thief until he walks through the detector beam, when the floodlights will light up. These are much safer and better for a horse than leaving floodlights on all night glaring out into the field.

Deterrents

There are certain physical deterrents that an owner can use to safeguard his horse. The best known amongst these is freezemarking, where a permanent mark is applied to the horse's skin, using a chilled branding iron. Contrary to popular belief, it does not hurt a horse, and should not affect his chances in the show ring. The mark is applied to a clipped area of the horse's back on the saddle patch, and the pigment cells in the hair are destroyed, growing back white within a few weeks. Grey or light coloured horses are marked in the same way, but the mark stays bald; for this reason, the area on grey horses may need regular clipping so the freezemark is clearly visible. If a horse is sold on, he will be easier to trace if he is freezemarked. Many insurance companies offer premium reductions if it has been done, as the chances of tracing a stolen horse without a freezemark are slim. Owners should remember to keep the hair over the freezemark clipped off during the winter, otherwise it may be harder to make out. Another good tip is to paint the freezemark over the top of the horse's rug; this leaves a thief in no doubt as to what is underneath, and may deter him from taking a marked horse. It is also a good way of identifying your rugs if they are stolen – or 'borrowed' by other owners in a livery yard.

Other deterrents available to the horse owner include:

- Hoof branding, a painless technique where the farrier burns an identification code – often the owner's postcode – into a horse's hooves. This form of identification needs to be re-done at least twice a year, as the brand will grow out with the hoof.

- Identichipping is another means of identifying a horse. A small microchip is injected under the horse's skin, carrying an identification code. When scanned, the chip is revealed and the code traced via a scanner network. Though not visible to a thief, this form of identification is very useful. The network of scanners encompasses all major sale rings, and also slaughter houses where the meat is sold for human consumption. Horsewatch co-ordinators and crime prevention officers are also aware of this method of identifying stolen horses, and scanners are supplied on free loan to other establishments and personnel who require them for possible identification of lost or stolen horses. Notices are put on the field gates and fences to potential theives that the horses have been protected in this way, and there are also small tags which can be attached to the headcollar.

A freezemark will definitely reduce the chances of your horse being stolen, as such horses are easily traceable

HEALTH & VET

Normal Parameters
Knowing your horse
Temperature, pulse and
   respiration

Routine Care & Attention
Best of health
Bots
Preventing disease
Tooth trouble
Recognising the signs of ill
   health
Sick nursing
Administering injections

First Aid
On the spot
The first-aid kit
Wound cleaning
Bandaging awkward areas
When to call the vet

Coping with Emergencies
Shock waves
Confident in a crisis
Choke
Eye injuries

Problems in the Foot
Hot spots
Splits and cracks
Punctured soles

Thrush
Seedy toe
Bruised soles
Laminitis
Pedal ostitis
Recognising navicular

Problems in the Leg
Common leg problems
Lymphangitis

Problems in the Body Structure
Azoturia
Managing arthritis

Problems of the Intestine
Colic
Diarrhoea

Skin Problems
Mucking about in mud
Sweet itch
Ringworm
Tack injuries

Coping with Viral Infections
Flu
Viruses

Old Age
The final decision

Part 3:
ERINARY CARE

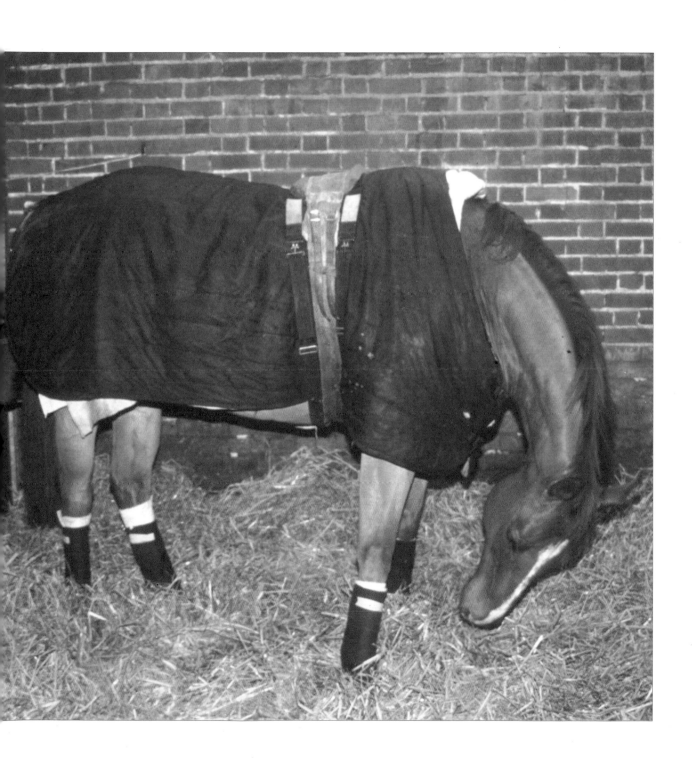

Knowing your horse

PROBLEM Looking after a horse is a great responsibility as well as a pleasure, but sometimes it can all seem a bit daunting. This may be especially true if an owner has not grown up with horses around, or had any formal equestrian training. So how can he learn the skills and acquire the knowledge in order to look after his horse's health and well-being, especially if he has other commitments such as a full-time job or a family?

SOLUTION The key to keeping a horse healthy is 'knowing the horse', and this is something that doesn't take any scientific qualifications. Getting to know a horse really well is the most important factor in establishing a good, knowledgeable relationship.

If an owner has taken the time to get to know his horse really well, he will be able to tell within a few minutes of greeting him whether or not the horse is feeling well, and will be the first to detect when it is acting oddly; it's like a sixth sense: he may not be able to pinpoint exactly what the problem is, but nevertheless he will know that the horse is 'not right'. This sixth sense is often like an early warning system to more serious illnesses, so it is a great asset for an owner to acquire. However, if he doesn't really know what constitutes normal behaviour for his horse, then it may take longer for him to realise when it is not in full health.

Such early detection may prevent many ailments from turning

Equestrian Home Study courses may prove helpful to the busy horse owner

into more serious conditions if they are treated promptly and correctly, and immediate and efficient first aid can produce quicker and superior healing and recovery. An owner should therefore know how to deal with minor ailments and have enough knowledge to cope with a situation until expert help arrives – and while this does mean knowing what should be done, it often more importantly means knowing what should not.

Where time and commitments prevent an owner from taking a course at a recognised training yard or equestrian centre, he may gain considerable knowledge from books and magazines. There are also equestrian home study courses that may prove helpful. However, such theoretical knowledge should be put into practice at every given opportunity, so an owner should practise techniques for bandaging, dressing wounds and suchlike, long before he may ever need to use them.

Temperature, pulse and respiration (TPR)

SOLUTION **Taking the temperature** A horse's normal temperature is 100.5°F (37.9°C), although a variation up or down of about half a degree is normal. A vet should always be called if a horse's temperature rises above 101.5°F (38.6°C), or falls below 100°F. To take a horse's temperature procede as follows:

- Shake down the mercury so that it is well below 100°F (37.8°C); with a digital thermometer the exact temperature will be provided without it having to be read.
- Lubricate the bulb of the thermometer with petroleum jelly.
- Lift the horse's tail, and standing to the side, insert the bulb of the thermometer into the horse's rectum at a slight angle for at least one minute, being sure to hold the end securely.
- Remove the thermometer and read instantly, wiping clean first if necessary.
- The thermometer should be disinfected immediately after use to prevent the spread of any infection.

Taking the pulse To take the pulse the owner should feel under the horse's upper jaw (the part that is semi-circular in shape) until he comes to the softness of an artery. This particular artery is know as the maxillary artery and is usually the easiest from which to record the pulse. At the place where the artery crosses the jaw, a definite beat can be felt. If the horse is generally fit and well his pulse rate at rest will be in the region of 35 to 40 beats per minute. If this rate exceeds 50 at rest, the cause needs to be investigated further.

Taking the respiration rate The simplest way to do this is by placing a hand over one of the horse's nostrils and then counting the breaths felt within a minute. While at rest your horse's respiration rate should be between eight and twelve breaths per minute, and they should be even and regular.

PROBLEM If visual checks and observations of the horse (see page 53) lead an owner to believe that it is off colour, the temperature, pulse and respiration are the next things to check. How are these taken, and what are normal and abnormal values?

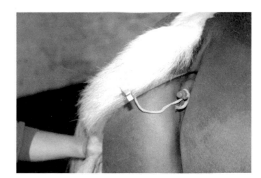

A good safety precaution is to fix one end of a piece of string securely onto the end of the thermometer and the other onto a peg which is then clipped onto the horse's tail. If for any reason you accidentally let go of the thermometer, and this safety precaution is not being employed, it might never be seen again!

Best of health

PROBLEM   What routine treatments and care should be carried out to ensure a horse stays in the best of health?

SOLUTION   An owner will have the best chance of keeping his horse healthy if he:

■ provides the horse with a balanced diet relating to the amount of exercise it receives, and to its size and metabolism (the total of the horse's chemical and physical activities)

■ ensures that the horse receives basic routine care such as regular worming, vaccinations, foot care and dentistry

■ always endeavours to allow his horse plenty of time out of its stable. It should be turned out as much as possible, and if kept in for any length of time, it should have plenty of walks in hand. While this may prove time-consuming a horse's mental health will soon start to suffer if it is shut up all day long, and this will in turn affect its overall health.

■ Most horses need worming every six to eight weeks, although this does depend on certain individual factors, such as whether the horse is stabled or lives at grass with other horses.

■ To protect against equine influenza and tetanus a horse will need vaccinating. This entails a veterinary surgeon coming to give a horse an initial course of two injections, followed by yearly boosters. A vaccination certificate will be issued by the veterinary surgeon to

Worming should be carried out on average every six to eight weeks

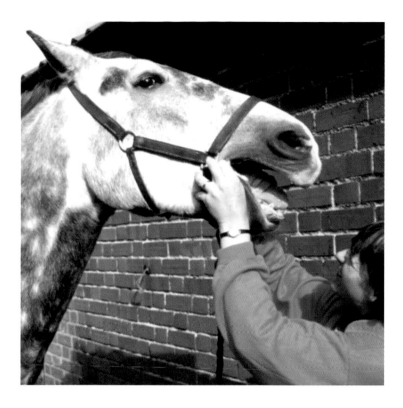

prove that a horse has been vaccinated, and racecourses and many shows require owners to produce this certificate before they will allow the horse access to the ground.

■ A horse's teeth will probably need rasping once a year, although if he is under four or over sixteen years of age then he may need more regular check-ups.

■ If the horse is in work he will probably need shoeing about every five or six weeks. If unshod he will need to be trimmed every six to eight weeks.

Such routine care should reduce the need for first aid because the healthy horse is less likely to succumb to disease, infection or injury.

Bots

PROBLEM What are the little yellow specks that can be seen on a horse's legs and body during the summer months, and do they harm the horse in any way?

SOLUTION These yellow flecks are bot fly eggs which are laid onto a horse's skin, usually on the lower limbs, so that when the horse licks himself, he will take the eggs into his body on his tongue. These parasites only use the horse's hair and skin as a means of entry into the horse's body. The eggs then develop into fully fledged worms inside the body. The yellow eggs should be removed from the legs with a bot fly comb and a good stiff brush as soon as they appear, and every owner should ensure his horse's worming programme is adhered to.

Preventing disease

PROBLEM While there are many things that cannot be avoided, sometimes illness is preventable if an owner is at all times vigilant and responsible in his attitude towards, and his care of his own horse and other horses in a yard. What practical things can an owner do to help prevent disease and illness?

SOLUTION Routine vaccinations will help to prevent diseases, but all horses in a yard should be covered. Rules of cleanliness should also be observed, and strict attention paid to such routine matters as:

- **grooming** – having wiped the horse's dock with a clean sponge, the same sponge should not be used on his eyes and nostrils.
- **dealing with minor ailments** – scurfy skin and grazes should be attended to as soon as they appear, as this often prevents them from turning into more nasty conditions which can then take considerably longer to deal with.

Good stable management is of paramount importance in the prevention of disease, as poor management is known to be a major contributing factor to the origin of many diseases. Thus if a horse does develop an ailment the owner should always ask himself 'Could this have been avoided?' While it might not make him feel too good if, in all honesty, his answer is 'yes', it will at least prevent him from making the same mistake again.

Scurfy skin such as this provides a haven for mites, lice and bacterial infections

---

TIP

In order to prevent suffering an owner must be vigilant, and should evaluate his horse each day in all situations. In particular he should think about whether:

- the horse is his normal self;
- anything happened yesterday that may have affected him;
- his nose and eyes are free from discharge;
- his skin is free from sores;
- his feet and limbs are in good order;
- his shoes are on tight;
- he is quite happy and sound when ridden;
- he is sweating unusually;
- he is eating up as normal.

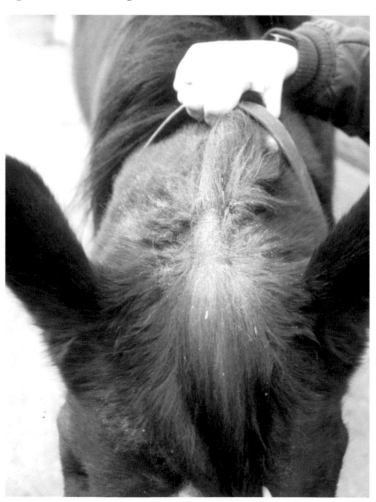

Tooth trouble

SOLUTION Many owners shy away from routinely inspecting their horse's mouth; probably because a horse's teeth are large and numerous, and they don't like the thought of a nasty bite! In addition, a horse might not like his mouth being inspected, so 'out of sight, out of mind' is often the easier option.

Luckily it is possible to check a horse's teeth for signs of sharpness from the outside of the face. An owner should feel the horse's cheek where the ridge of teeth jut out and run the fingers firmly down the line of teeth. A sharp edge may not be felt, but if the horse objects to the pressure then this is a good indication that his teeth need rasping, and even that his cheek may be sore.

Other signs which may indicate that a horse's teeth need attention include:

- quidding, when he continually drops food from his mouth while eating;
- slow eating;
- loss of condition, which could be caused as a result of improperly chewed food;
- whole grains of food in the droppings;
- signs of impaction colic;
- ridden evasions such as nodding, leaning on one rein, going behind or above the bit and in more severe cases even rearing, napping and bolting.

Rasping a horse's teeth is not a job an owner can do himself , as it takes a great deal of knowledge and expertise. Either a veterinary surgeon should do it, or someone who is experienced at tooth rasping and has been highly recommended by a reliable source.

Neglected teeth at the very least can cause a horse pain, and at worst may mean he needs dental surgery which is both expensive and formidable: there are problems with access, and a horse's teeth are also very firmly attached to the jaw, making removal a major undertaking. The most certain way of ensuring no tooth problems are neglected is to have them checked on a regular basis every six to twelve months.

PROBLEM It is an owner's responsibility to ensure that his horse does not suffer any unnecessary pain in his mouth. Many problems are concealed, and poor performance or condition caused by tooth trouble tends to creep up gradually. How can an owner be sure that his horse does not have any tooth problems, and what should be done if problems are encountered?

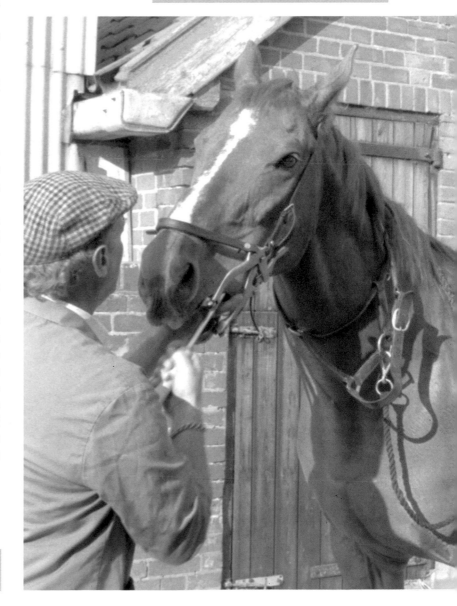

Only a professional should rasp a horse's teeth: it takes a great deal of knowledge and expertise

Recognising the signs of ill health

PROBLEM   If a horse is feeling off-colour he will generally appear listless, and it is to be hoped that his owner will recognise that all is not as it should be. What physical signs might an owner look for to confirm illness before calling a veterinary surgeon?

SOLUTION   Physical signs of ill health can include:

A change of colour in the eye membranes

Pale membranes might indicate that a horse is suffering from anaemia, chronic indigestion or worms. Deep red membranes are a sign that he is running a fever, whereas red membranes with a blue tinge indicate pneumonia. Yellow membranes might indicate a disorder of the liver, and blue-red membranes are indicative of heart and circulatory problems.

A change in a horse's coat

If it is standing on end – 'staring' – and dull in appearance, then this is often a good indication that a horse may be malnourished or ill. Also if his mane can be pulled out easily, then this might also indicate ill health.

A change in the skin

Certain changes in the skin are often a warning of illness or distress. Generally if a horse is in ill health then his skin will tighten up – the owner will notice it does not move freely back and forth as it should. This may indicate that he is in the early stages of a general disease; or he may have lice; or he may just be generally malnourished. The pinch test (see page 125) should be carried out to see whether or not the skin springs back into place.

Signs of sweating

While excessive sweating may be caused by too much exercise if a horse is unfit, or by nervousness or excitement, the cause should be evident to the owner. If, however, a horse breaks out into a sudden cold sweat unexpectedly while at rest then he may be in acute physical pain or suffering from some form of mental imbalance, and you should take steps to find out what is wrong as soon as possible. An uncharacteristic hot sweat is often a clear indication that a horse has a fever.

Puffy or swollen limbs

Puffy limbs can denote ill health for various conditions. If the puffiness is due to a bone or joint problem then a horse will obviously be lame. If his limbs are generally puffy all over then he might be suffering from heart trouble or a digestive problem. Localised puffiness may indicate that he has a skin irritation or has suffered an injury.

Sick nursing

PROBLEM   When a horse becomes ill he will need more care than normal. How can an owner be sure that he is satisfying both the physical and mental needs of the horse, thus helping him to make as speedy a recovery as possible?

SOLUTION   An ill horse needs to be kept warm and dry. If he is normally turned out, he should be brought in so that a close eye can be kept on him, and if he is cold he will need rugging up in order to maintain a normal body temperature. A horse's temperature is something an owner can check straight away, because if a vet needs to be called he will find it most helpful if he knows whether or not the horse is running a temperature before he arrives. Horses suffering from shock in particular will need to be kept warm, and artificial heaters, preferably infra-red ones, may be needed for this. The horse's bed should be well banked up, dry and clean, although bedding should not be shaken up while the horse is still in the stable as this may irritate him and make him cough.

If an ill horse has lost his appetite, and providing food is not contra-indicated by the vet, he should be encouraged to eat by adding succulents such as carrots, sugar beet or molasses to his feed. Ask your vet about adding electrolytes to his water, which will also help to maintain essential body salts. The horse should be walked out as soon as he is able, to provide at least some exercise, and he should be turned out as soon as the vet advises.

The owner should maintain high standards of hygiene to ensure he does not inadvertently pass on any infectious diseases. If a horse has any noticeable discharges, these should be cleaned away with a fresh sponge and clean, tepid water. Fresh air is also essential: while an ill horse needs to be kept warm – unless he is running a high temperature – the top door of his stable should not be closed at any time. However, the owner should ensure that his stable is free from draughts and has good air circulation.

An ill horse's condition needs constant assessment. He should be checked over regularly, and this should include readings being taken of his TPR, and the veterinary surgeon should be informed of any change.

Succulents may help to tempt a sick horse to eat

An ailing horse needs to be kept warm and dry in a calm, quiet and familiar environment

Administering injections

PROBLEM If an owner has never given a horse an injection, the possible necessity of doing so might make him a little apprehensive. Many owners never give injecting techniques a thought because it is the veterinary surgeon who always gives a horse his vaccinations, but what if their horse were to become ill and he needed an injection every day? What procedure should they follow when giving a horse an injection?

WARNING

Injections given by persons other than veterinary surgeons should only be intramuscular.

TIP

The moment of actually inserting the needle is when many horse owners freeze. If this happens they should stay calm and endeavour to count one, two, three, and on 'three' tell themselves that they are going to put the needle in.

There are three normal ways of giving an injection:
- intramuscular, where the fluid is placed into the muscle tissue;
- subcutaneous, where the fluid is placed under the skin;
- intravenous, where the fluid goes directly into the bloodstream through a vein.

TECHNIQUE The following step-by-step method is quick and easy.

1. The injection site must be dry and free from dirt. The hands should be washed thoroughly and the injection site swabbed with surgical or methylated spirits.

2. Check that the right drug has been chosen and read the instructions on the bottle carefully, noting the expiry date and batch number. The bottle should be shaken vigorously and the rubber bottle stopper swabbed with surgical or methylated spirit (a).

3. Unpack a sterile needle and place it onto a sterile syringe with the needle cover still on. Remove this cover, and with the drug bottle upside-down, insert the needle through the rubber into the fluid.

4. Hold the syringe tightly with the thumb and forefinger, and withdraw the plunger until the syringe is filled with slightly more of the drug than is required (b). Pull the needle out of the bottle while still in the upright position. Tap the syringe to encourage any tiny air bubbles to rise. Then push the plunger until a few drips of the drug flow down the needle to ensure there is no air in the syringe. Extract the needle from the syringe.

5. Holding the needle between the thumb and the first two fingers, tap the horse firmly with the base of the fist close to the sterile injection site (c). This prepares the horse so that he does not jump suddenly when the needle is inserted.

6. Insert the needle purposefully, so that it goes in up to the plastic base (d). It is important to be sure that no blood seeps from the needle, as this indicates that it has hit a blood vessel. If this does happen, the needle should be extracted quickly and re-inserted in a slightly different position.

7. Attach the drug-filled syringe (e) and pull back the plunger minutely to ensure no blood enters the syringe. Push the plunger in slowly to administer the drug. Sometimes the plunger needs to be pushed quite hard (this all depends on the density of the fluid being injected) and it is a sensible precaution to hold the point at which the needle and syringe join as they can be forced apart if the fluid is particularly thick.

8. Using a steady pressure the plunger is pushed in until all the fluid has gone (f). Do not be alarmed if a slight bump appears at the injection site. Withdraw the needle quickly and purposefully. A few drops of blood may appear at this point, but this is nothing to worry about. Do not pat the horse strongly on the injection site, although a gentle rub with the base of the fist seems to be soothing.

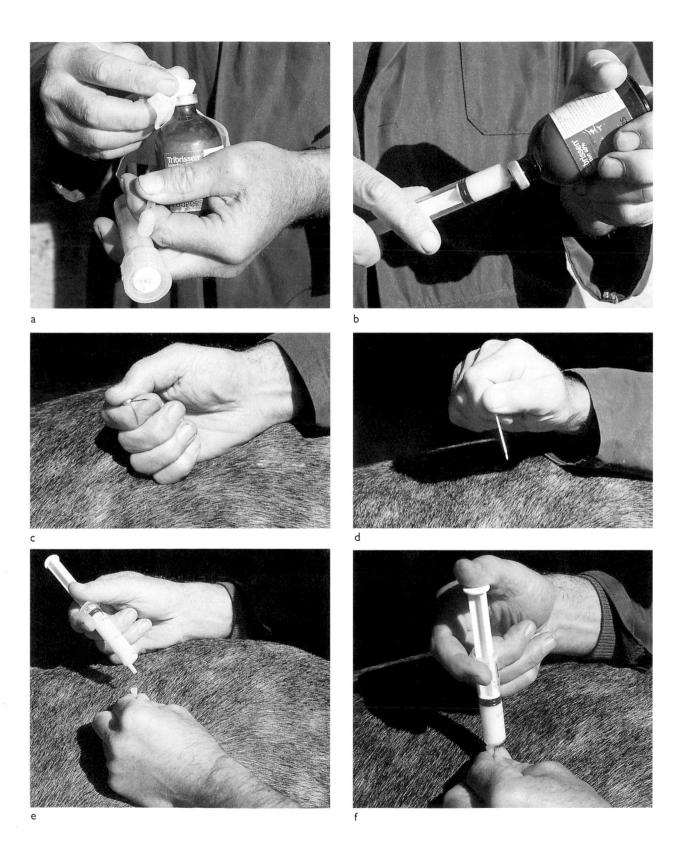

a

b

c

d

e

f

On the spot

PROBLEM Who is the best person to administer first aid? Should the horse's owner do what he can to help the horse, or should it all be left until a qualified veterinary surgeon arrives?

SOLUTION The best person to administer first aid is the person who is on the spot. If in doubt about an illness or injury an owner should, of course, call a veterinary surgeon; however, he may take an hour or so to arrive and the time spent administering correct first aid while waiting can often be the 'make or break' of a sick horse's recovery.

First aid means giving the horse immediate attention to prevent a more serious illness from occurring, or dealing with the horse until the vet can attend. Second aid entails the continuing treatment of an illness, and this will involve both the horse's owner and the horse's vet. Even though an owner may have administered first aid successfully, the importance of seeking veterinary help for a correct diagnosis to be made, or as 'second aid' when necessary, should never be forgotten. It is important that owners learn to work with their horse's vet: while correct first aid is essential, it will not replace the need for veterinary attention, but it will help to keep vets' bills to a minimum.

Every owner is more than likely to find himself at some stage having to cope with an emergency, or a situation which requires immediate action. Coping with the unexpected is far easier if the correct procedures to follow are known (see also page 99), and everyday cuts and bruises, which if neglected might lead to nasty complications will benefit from immediate, efficient care. Every owner needs to acquire both the knowledge that will help to keep his horse healthy, and the skills to tackle common problems.

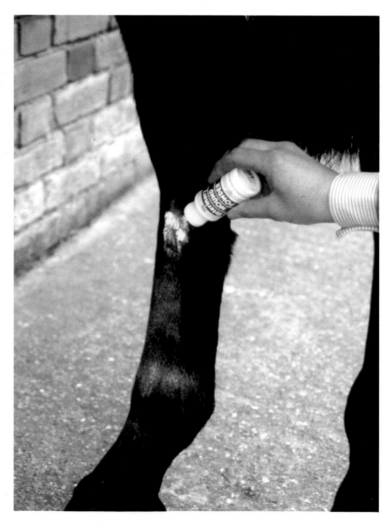

The first-aid kit

SOLUTION Commercial first-aid kits contain all an owner might need for instant first aid, and these are ideal when travelling. However, any owner can quite easily make up a first-aid kit of his own, and its contents should include:

- a 12in (30cm) roll of gamgee tissue – an absorbent, cushioned wadding for infected and discharging wounds, which also provides leg support;

PROBLEM In order to cope with the day-to-day responsibilities of administering first aid when necessary, every owner should have a properly equipped first-aid kit and a back-up medicine cupboard. What should a first-aid kit contain?

Check your first-aid kit regularly to ensure it is well stocked

- two packets of Animalintex dressing – for poulticing;
- veterinary antiseptic spray – for the treatment of superficial wounds;
- veterinary wound powder – for use on minor wounds, sores, cuts, bites and scratches;
- waterproof sticking plaster – for securing bandages;
- bandages, 2in (5cm) and 3in (7.5cm) wide – for securing dressings and providing support;
- a packet of antiseptic lint – for use on open wounds;
- a jar of ordinary salt – for use diluted with water as a wash, and to help harden skin;
- a packet of Epsom salts – for use as a laxative;
- vaseline – for use when taking a horse's temperature;
- a small bottle of iodine – to counter irritants;
- a cold pack – for application to bruised or damaged tendons;
- disposable syringes and needles – for when injections are needed;
- a tube of antiseptic skin ointment – for wounds, sores and bites;
- a veterinary thermometer – to take the horse's temperature;
- a pair of scissors – these should be sharp but blunt-ended, and are used for cutting away hair from the edges of wounds or cuts that need dressing, and for cutting the dressing itself.

TIP

Every time an owner has cause to use something from the first-aid kit it should be replaced immediately as no one knows how soon that particular item will be needed again. Also, certain items such as medicines, creams and lotions can go out of date, so these need checking periodically and replacing when necessary. The seals on sterile materials should also be checked to ensure they are intact; if not they should not be used, but should be replaced.

Wound cleaning

PROBLEM What should an owner do if he finds his horse in the field or stable one morning with a wound? How should he clean it, and should the wound be dressed, or left in the open to dry and drain?

SOLUTION All wounds, however minor, should be cleaned thoroughly if they are to have the best possible chance of healing quickly and well. Very often the flow of blood itself is enough to clean the wound. If dirt is visible in minor wounds, it can be carefully removed and the wound further cleaned with a swab soaked in warm salty water (about one teaspoon of salt to one pint/half a litre of water). Using a clean swab each time, the owner should work from the middle of the wound outwards so that no dirt is taken back into the wound. If dirt is still present it is usually sufficient to run a hosepipe above the area, so that a gentle trickle of water removes any dirt and congealed blood. At this stage no pressure should be used from the hose as this may push dirt further into the wound.

After cleaning, minor cuts should be left to dry and then treated sparingly with an antiseptic powder or spray. This process should be repeated three times daily until the wound has dried up and is mending well. However, if having cleaned the wound it becomes obvious that it needs stitching, it should be covered with a clean piece of gamgee, bandaged in place and the vet called. No healing creams, powders, sprays or gels should be administered before the vet arrives, as this will only hinder his assessment and treatment.

More serious wounds will need dressing, and badly infected wounds may need poulticing to draw out dirt and infection. If the wound is not infected, a lint wound-dressing such a Mellolin can be applied: this is put directly onto the wound, covered with a piece of gamgee and bandaged into place over another layer of gamgee which extends all the way down the leg. Such dressings need changing twice daily until the wound has scabbed over.

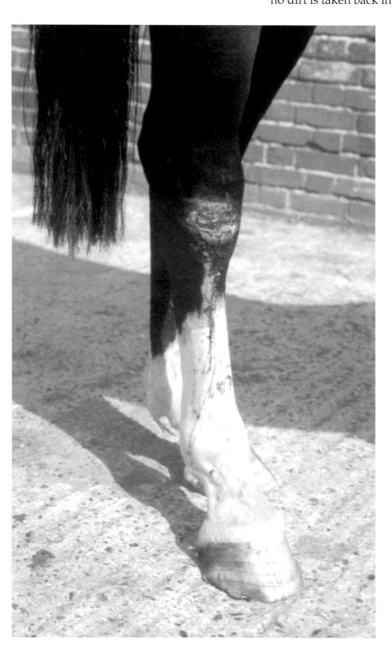

Cleaning a wound from the inside to the outer edges is important to avoid further problems arising from contamination by dirt entering the wound

Bandaging awkward areas

SOLUTION The forearm is a common site of injury but it is difficult to keep a dressing in place on it. An owner should start by dressing and bandaging as normal, but should not go below the top of the knee with the bandage. The bandage should not be too tight, and the pressure must be even all the way down. The biggest problem with bandaging in this area is preventing it from slipping down. A strip of sticking plaster may be required around the upper part of the bandage to prevent this, although it must be applied no more tightly than the bandage itself.

When bandaging knees and hocks, a figure-of-eight technique should be used. Plenty of padding is put around the joint, and bandaged in place using a slightly elasticated or self adhesive bandage. When done correctly, the bandage forms a cross at the front of the knee and the back of knee is not covered by the bandage at all, which still allows the knee to bend. When bandaging the hock, the reverse procedure is followed so that the point of the hock has the cross over it and the front is left uncovered.

PROBLEM Bandaging lower limbs is a fairly straightforward process with which few owners have difficulty. Unfortunately however, wounds may be in places which are more difficult to keep a bandage on. What techniques can an owner use to ensure that on awkward areas bandages stay where they are put?

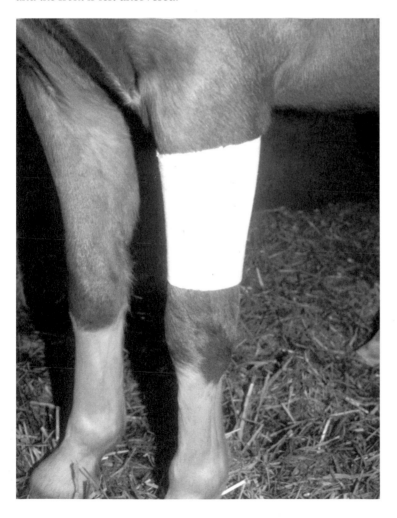

'Tubigrip' provides an excellent alternative when in need of securing a dressing in areas such as the knee or hock. It is pulled on like a stocking and can simply be folded up whilst changing the dressing and cleaning the wound, and folded back down again once a clean dressing is in place. To enable movement of the joints, a gap can be cut out over prominent bones.

When to call the vet

PROBLEM   When an owner administers first aid, even for the most minor problems, he undertakes certain responsibilities. First, he must assess the condition of the horse and identify the main problem, and while the problem may seem obvious it is often wise to double check. How does an owner decide whether or not a veterinary surgeon's expertise is required?

SOLUTION   A veterinary surgeon should be called if:
■ there is an obvious reason for doing so, such as colic or lameness;
■ a horse deviates from his normal behaviour and his owner cannot understand why – if neither his feed nor his exercise routine has not been changed, for example;
■ he is needed to back up an owner's first aid, by stitching a wound, for example;
■ a horse is due to receive his vaccinations or other general health maintenance checks, such as rasping his teeth;
■ an owner is in doubt whether the horse needs to see him or not. The vet may be able to put an owner's mind at rest on the telephone, or he may make the decision to come out. In such cases it is far better to be over-cautious.

An owner can help the vet by keeping a clear record of what he has found and what he has done, so the vet can take this into account when deciding further treatment.

The knowledgeable owner should be capable of dealing with minor injuries, but more serious cuts and illnesses, like this, are a job for the veterinary surgeon

PROBLEM Should a horse be involved in an accident or a frightening situation, he is likely to go into shock. How can an owner check if his horse is in shock, and what can he do until the vet arrives?

SOLUTION To check whether a horse is in shock the owner should first assess whether he appears depressed and dazed; the coat should also be felt to see whether it is cold to touch. If shock is suspected the owner should:

- take the horse's temperature – it may be lower than normal;
- take a look at the horse's mucous membranes – they may have taken on a bluish tinge;
- take the horse's pulse – it may be rapid – but weak.

A vet must be called at once. Immediate action while waiting involves getting the horse into a nice warm stable and putting on dry rugs and stable bandages, or if possible turning on infra-red lights to keep the horse warm.

> *A horse does not necessarily need to have been in an emergency to suffer from shock, there are many other causes such as colic, diarrhoea or severe injury which can also result in shock, so it pays to be vigilant at all times.*

> *A horse in shock needs immediate veterinary attention; while waiting for the vet to arrive, the owner can help keeping the horse warm and keeping a record of his temperature, condition of the mucous membranes, and pulse*

Confident in a crisis

PROBLEM What should an owner do if he finds a horse bleeding from a cut: should he call the vet, or try to stop the bleeding himself?

SOLUTION Wounds can vary enormously in their degree of severity, and this will govern the action to be taken. A minor wound will usually stop by itself within a few minutes, but a more serious one will need immediate action. The danger of infection exists with any wound, so it is important to ensure that a horse has regular tetanus boosters.

Immediate action

If bright red blood can be seen spurting out of a wound, then a horse may have severed an artery, in which case the first priority is to stop the flow of blood. If blood is obviously coming from a single artery, pressure using the thumb should be applied about an inch along the

The first priority is to stem the flow of blood by using a pressure pad directly over the wound

---

artery above the wound, to arrest the flow. If this does not work, a pad of clean material (gamgee is fine if it is ready to hand) should be held firmly over the wound and again pressure applied. If possible someone else should call the vet immediately, telling him what is happening. If the owner is alone and so must leave the horse in order to call the vet, the pad should be firmly bandaged in place and the owner must return without delay – his only thought at this stage should be to stop the blood flow. Pressure must be sustained on the pad. If blood soaks through the pad, this should not be removed for a new one, but another gamgee pad should simply be applied over the top. Once the bleeding has slowed, the pad/s can be bandaged firmly and evenly over the area until the vet arrives or treatment can proceed.

Choke

PROBLEM

This is a condition where food has caused an obstruction in the horse's oesophagus (throat). What are the various signs which might alert an owner to the condition, and what action should be taken?

SOLUTION

The signs of choke are as follows:

- uneasiness and difficulty in swallowing;
- coughing to try to remove the obstruction;
- contracting and extending the neck;
- making low grunting sounds;
- box walking;
- green-brown fluid dripping down the nostrils;
- drooling at the mouth;
- rubbing the head and neck.

Immediate action

If an owner finds his horse showing these signs, he should wait for ten minutes to see if the obstruction passes of its own accord, which in many cases it will. If the horse is not in a stable, he should be brought in away from other horses; he should not be given anything to eat or drink. If after ten minutes he has not recovered, a vet should be called forthwith, as the horse may need an injection to relax him and so allow the obstruction to disperse more easily. Sometimes it may be necessary to pass a stomach tube down the horse's throat to clear the blockage.

After the blockage has cleared, a horse's throat may be a little sore so only soft mashes should be given for a few days; also he should be allowed to eat grass in preference to hay, which if there is no alternative must be soaked.

Prevention

While there is little an owner can do to remedy the situation once it has occurred, he can take preventative measures. Usually choke occurs when a greedy horse comes into the stable to be fed, having been out all day; typically he will dive into his feeding trough and devour his feed rapidly, not waiting to chew it up properly. Within seconds he can be showing signs of choke, and it will depend on how bad the blockage is as to how quickly it will pass, or whether it will need veterinary attention. Sometimes the blockage may only be an inch or so in length, and if the horse had consumed most of his feed before the blockage occurred, this will pass into the stomach and be digested as normal. But if the blockage occurs from the first mouthful, the horse may continue to eat until he can physically eat no longer, and the food just stacks up in front of the blockage. It is often possible to feel a hard mass of food along the throat in such cases.

- First the owner should try to establish whether his horse is greedy because he is hungry, or just plain greedy! If a horse is hungry when coming in from the field, he is not getting enough sustenance from the grazing, so he should be supplied with hay while in the field.
- If feeding in the field with other horses, the bowls should be placed far apart (see also page 58) so that he doesn't feel threatened, because this in itself will encourage him to bolt his food.
- A horse's feed should not be put into his stable before he is brought in – he should be brought in and allowed some time to munch at his hay before he is given his concentrate feed.
- If he still dives into his food, then a salt lick can be placed on top of his food, which will make him slow down.
- Chaff should be included in his feed to encourage him to chew his food up properly before swallowing.
- An owner should always ensure that sugar beet is soaked for twenty-four hours before feeding, and should consider changing from nuts to mixes if a horse has suffered from choke on more than one occasion.
- Be sure to cut up carrots and apples lengthways, and not into round pieces or cubes which might become lodged in the throat.
- An owner should check regularly that the horse's teeth don't need rasping, or that he doesn't have gum disease or sores in his mouth, as a sore mouth may prevent him from chewing his food properly.

Horse showing signs of choke

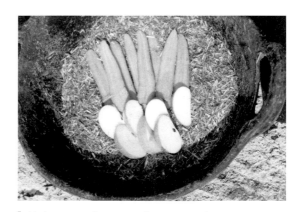

Make sure that succulents are always cut lengthways

Eye injuries

PROBLEM One of the biggest problems with the eyes is that they are rather prominent on each side of the horse's head and so are particularly susceptible to knocks and the ingress of foreign bodies, which trauma often leads to infection. What can an owner do if his horse has got something in his eye?

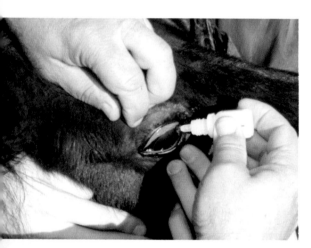

Applying eye drops must be done swiftly and very carefully

TIP

The signs which act as a warning to an eye problem are often quite obvious. Examination should involve the following questions, and the information should be relayed to the veterinary surgeon:

- *is there any discharge?*
- *is there any swelling?*
- *have the eyelids suffered any injury, however small?*
- *does the horse insist on keeping his eyes shut?*
- *has the colour of the eye altered – has it become cloudy or dull?*
- *does the horse object to bright light?*
- *does he show any signs of blindness?*

SOLUTION If something does enter the horse's eye, action must be taken quickly to prevent further suffering. First, the offending object needs to be removed gently, either by picking out with clean fingers (no long nails) if clearly visible, or by flushing out with cooled, boiled water. Conjunctivitis – inflammation of the conjunctiva, the membrane covering the inside of the eyelids – may follow as a result of such a problem. In such cases an owner needs to give first aid by administering eye ointment or drops. The horse may be less than enthusiastic about this, so to ensure best results, everything should be prepared in advance so as to be able to proceed in a methodical manner.

Step-by-step treatment

- Someone must hold the horse, because treating the eye is impossible to do alone.
- Hands should be washed thoroughly.
- The ointment or drops should be warmed to body temperature by standing in a bowl of warm water for a few minutes – but be careful not to overheat them. The nozzle of the tube or pipette must be clean and free from contamination.
- With some warm and moist cotton wool, wipe away any discharge which may have collected in the corner of the eye.
- With the dropper or tube held between the thumb and first two fingers, rest the heel of the hand against the horse's cheek.
- With the other hand gently but swiftly turn the horse's eyelid outwards and immediately squeeze in the drops, or apply a line of ointment between eyeball and eyelid.
- Every effort must be taken not to touch the eyeball with the end of the pipette or tube, otherwise the horse may be even less likely to co-operate next time.

If for any reason easy access to the horse's eye cannot be gained, a veterinary surgeon must attend. If the eye is clearly stuck up with discharge or squeezed tightly shut due to pain, it must not be forced open; in such cases a topical anaesthesia is needed. The horse might find some relief if he is kept in a darkened area.

- There are other conditions which can affect the eye, ulcers for instance. These usually occur as a result of the cornea, the front part of the eyeball, being scratched or infected. These are treated in the same way, with drops or ointment from the veterinary surgeon. As long as such problems are noticed as soon as they appear and are treated promptly, they will usually clear up quite satisfactorily. If the response to treatment is not fairly rapid the vet should be called. In any event it is a sensible precaution to alert him to the problem and to explain how it is being treated. There is a far worse condition known as moon blindness, which if not promptly treated by a vet could cause blindness. This disease shows very similar symptoms to more common ailments.

Hot spots

PROBLEM How does an owner determine which hoof is causing a problem with lameness?

SOLUTION If a hoof-related problem is suspected, first the owner should feel for heat in the foot. To do this they should place their hand over the suspect hoof and hold it there until they can feel a constant temperature. Then the same hand is placed over the other hoof to see if there is any difference in temperature between the two.

If heat is detected, the horse should be trotted up on a level surface to see if he is lame. The handler should leave the horse's head loose: if he is lame in a forefoot, he will lift his head as the affected foot hits the ground; with the hind feet, he will drop his head as the affected foot touches the ground. Once heat in the foot has been established, a cause should be sought.

When checking for heat in the hooves, feel one foot and then the other in order to establish whether there is any difference between them

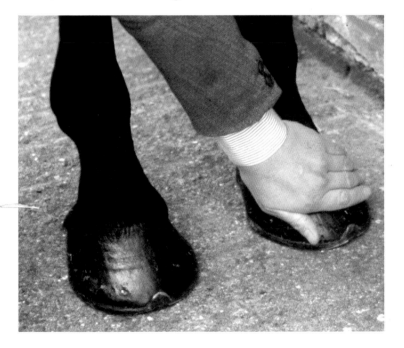

Splits and cracks

PROBLEM Cracks in the hoof wall are not usually emergencies, but they do need prompt attention if they are not to get worse and cause lameness. What can an owner do to treat split or cracked hooves, and is there anything he can do to prevent recurrence in the future?

SOLUTION Cracks in the hoof wall and dry, brittle feet go hand in hand and are the greatest cause of horses casting shoes. There are two main types of cracks: those which start at the ground and work upwards, known as grass cracks, and those which start at the coronary band and work downwards, known as sandcracks.

In the majority of cases the cracks only involve the horn, and as long as they are attended to promptly and correctly a horse should remain sound. If a horse goes lame, then it is likely that the crack goes deeper into the sensitive tissues of the hoof, known as the laminae, or that it has become infected. In some cases pus may be seen oozing out of the hoof, in which case it will need to be drained completely before any corrective action can be taken by a vet or farrier.

A farrier will be able to assist in the healing of a superficial crack by burning a groove at the top of the crack, or using a clip, to stop it travelling any further up or down the hoof. However, to help promote healthy hoof growth in the future there are various measures an owner can take – although patience will be required, as it can take up to a year for a horse to grow a completely new hoof.

- First, an owner should ensure that his horse's feet are kept well trimmed, and that his farrier does a good job – if he is not satisfied or has any particular worries, he should not be afraid to discuss them with him.
- A good, balanced diet should be provided.

If the quality of a horse's feet is poor, his feed can be supplemented with biotin or a specifically formulated multi-compound supplement. Hoof dressing can be applied, but one should be chosen that is designed to help strengthen and improve the condition of brittle feet.

- Cornucrescine can be applied; this is specifically formulated to encourage hoof growth.
- In the summer months if conditions are dry, it is beneficial to stand the horse in a stream for about fifteen minutes, or alternatively hose his hooves; they can then be oiled, after they have dried, to prevent the loss of the moisture that has been absorbed. However, if hooves are oiled without having first been wetted (for long enough for the water to soak in) then moisture will be prevented from getting in at all.
- It is advisable to avoid riding over hard ground, or on the road too much, or in deep mud; however, exercise should not be stopped as this helps to promote healthy hoof growth.

Punctured soles

PROBLEM Puncture wounds to the foot are very common and are often caused by a horse standing on a sharp object, such as a nail or flint. What immediate action should an owner take to prevent infection and ensure a speedy recovery?

SOLUTION All puncture wounds should be taken seriously as the wound can heal over and/or become infected, creating pus that sooner or later forms a painful abscess. Tetanus is also a risk, so a vet should be called for all but the most superficial of such wounds.

Immediate action

An owner may be alerted to a punctured sole in two ways: either the horse will be hobbling along with an offending item still in his foot, or it will suddenly go very lame. Any visible object still in the foot should be removed immediately, being careful to prevent further damage, and the hole or 'prick' treated immediately and covered to prevent infection. To clean the affected sole any mud or dirt should be washed off and the foot then dipped into a solution of salt water or mild antiseptic to help kill any infection. The area should be kept clean by covering it for a few days, and the owner should check to make sure that no infection is present before turning the horse out again.

If the foot is infected the horse will definitely be lame, even though there may be no visible sign of anything entering the foot. The vet should be called, and he may need to cut a hole in the sole to allow the pus to drain out; in preparation for this the foot should be poulticed, as this will help to soften the sole and draw the pus, ready for paring (cutting away)

There are specially designed boots which can be used to keep a poultice on, and it is a good idea to have one of these as a stand-by.

Punctured sole – here you can see clearly where the nail has left a hole in the sole of the hoof

Thrush

PROBLEM It is often said that thrush is the result of poor stable management. Why is this, and what can the owner do to prevent it happening to his horse. And if it does, what is the treatment?

SOLUTION Thrush is a condition which usually occurs as a result of a horse being allowed to stand on dirty, wet bedding for long periods of time, especially where the feet are not picked out regularly. The frog appears spongy and wet, and there is a foul-smelling black discharge. In order to prevent the condition, an owner should keep his horse's bed dry and clean, and the feet should be picked out daily and washed out regularly.

The first step in treating the condition is to clear out the old bedding and keep the stable dry and clean in the future. The feet should then be cleaned and scrubbed out daily, and once dry an antiseptic spray should be applied to the affected area. To protect the foot from wet bedding, Stockholm tar can also be applied.

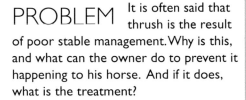

A hoof discharging a foul-smelling, black fluid: a sure sign of thrush

---

TIP

Thrush will usually clear up rapidly; if, however, the condition has been neglected to such an extent that the sensitive laminae have been affected, then the foot will need to be poulticed.

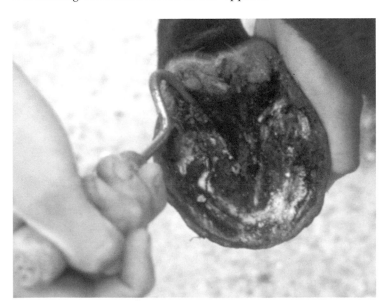

Seedy toe

PROBLEM What is seedy toe, how is it treated, and can it cause the horse to go lame?

SOLUTION Seedy toe is a hollow under the wall of the hoof, usually at the toe, where the sensitive laminae separate. The hollow is then filled up with crumbling horn which comes away easily on the end of a hoofpick. It is thought to have various causes but is often linked to infection or laminitis.

Initially a farrier will need to trim the toes. Then the owner should scrub out the hollow, pack it up with cotton wool and cover it with Stockholm tar. Alternatively the farrier can put a leather pad under the shoe to prevent dirt getting into the hollow, or he may use a substance which 'sets' into the hollow, thereby providing more stability.

Measures should be taken to promote healthy horn growth, as described for hoof cracks (see page 103).

Bruised soles

PROBLEM What are bruised soles, how are they caused and can they be avoided?

SOLUTION Bruised soles are a common cause of lameness usually resulting from a sharp object 'bruising' the bottom of the foot, through standing on a sharp stone, for example. In more severe cases the shoe will have to be removed and the foot examined, an abscess may result; this will need paring out by a vet or a farrier, and then poulticing. In some cases it is found that a corn (a bruise in the heel region) is the problem, in which case it will be cut out. A special surgical shoe may be fitted to relieve the pressure of corns.

If a horse is particularly thin-soled, it is sensible to ask the farrier about fitting a leather pad under the shoe.

A heart-bar shoe fittted to relieve the pressure of corns

Laminitis

SOLUTION Laminitis should always be treated as an emergency, as early treatment often leads to a more successful outcome.

Immediately laminitis is suspected, a veterinary surgeon should be called, and while awaiting his arrival the affected feet – which may be just one or up to all four – should be hosed to relieve the pain. Painkilling drugs should *not* be given before the vet arrives, as this will mask the severity of the condition.

PROBLEM Laminitis is a very painful condition notorious for afflicting ponies (and less frequently horses) grazing on lush spring grass. What are the symptoms to look out for, how should it be dealt with immediately, and what management is needed in the long term?

Muzzling a laminitic pony will help to prevent him from gorging on rich grass

---

SYMPTOMS OF LAMINITIS

There are certain symptoms which are typical to the laminitic condition:
- *the 'laminitic stance', where the horse stands with his forelegs stretched forwards;*
- *refusal to move;*
- *objection to having the sole tested with hoof pinchers;*
- *heat in the affected hoof/hooves;*
- *rings on the feet, indicating past attacks;*
- *a raised temperature, pulse and respiration rate caused by the pain.*

The cause of laminitis is very often too much grass or feed, and management of the condition necessitates restricting the grazing, either by putting the horse onto a piece of bare land with access to hay, or by muzzling him. The muzzle should be removed for at least one hour in every three depending on the severity of the condition, to allow restricted grazing. Alternatively, small holes can be cut into the bottom of a leather muzzle, allowing a few blades of grass to poke through at a time, thus making the horse work far harder for less food, while still providing ventilation and access to water.

It is essential to try and prevent the occurrence or recurrence of laminitis. As a long term measure, corrective trimming by an experienced remedial farrier will be necessary, as will special attention to exercise and diet in order to prevent obesity.

Pedal ostitis

PROBLEM Pedal ostitis is often said to be caused from laminitis. Is this true, and what symptoms should the owner be looking for?

SOLUTION This is a condition which affects the pedal bone in the horse's foot, and it may occur as a corollary to the horse having laminitis, or other foot problems. In very severe cases the pedal bone can rotate and come through the sole of the foot, so early diagnosis is essential.

An owner should look for:

- discomfort in both front feet;
- discomfort when being ridden on hard ground;
- relief when rested;
- signs of pain on testing the hoof with pincers.

This condition can only be diagnosed through a vet who will have access to certain equipment.

Recognising navicular

PROBLEM Mention the term 'navicular' and many horse owners turn cold. What is navicular, why does it frighten so many horse owners, and what can be done for a horse which suffers from it?

SOLUTION Navicular syndrome is a disease of the navicular bone in the horse's foot; it usually affects horses rather than ponies. It is an ostitis, and is due to pressure on the coffin bone when ulceration is caused. Concussion is the exciting cause of navicular. It is a degenerative disease and at the time of writing there is no known cure.

Symptoms which might lead an owner to believe that his horse has navicular include:

- stumbling and tripping up when ridden;
- a shuffling gait and shortened strides;
- standing with one or other fore toe pointed forwards;
- intermittent lameness;
- lame when lunged on a circle;
- shifting his weight from one foot to the other when standing still;
- boxy-looking hooves.

There are many treatments aimed at prolonging the working life of the horse, but none, as yet, to cure him. These include corrective farriery, drugs and de-nerving, a surgical operation to take away the pain in order that the horse is no longer lame. An owner should seek veterinary help as soon as the condition is suspected particularly as all of the above symptoms could be caused by some other condition; only X-rays will provide a definite diagnosis. If the horse does have navicular then it is only fair that he receives some form of pain relief.

Common leg problems

SOLUTION An owner should learn to recognise minor leg problems for what they are; he may like to have the vet to check them if they seem to be troubling the horse, but otherwise he should be able to deal with them himself. Common problems include:

PROBLEM There are many very common leg problems which affect horses. How does an owner learn to recognise them, and can he deal with them himself?

Swellings

These usually occur as a result of a horse knocking himself while out in the field, or when rolling in the stable. A certain amount of bruising occurs, and the owner should try to disperse this as quickly as possible. Heat can usually be felt at the site of the swelling, so applying cold treatment as soon as possible will help. After a day or so alternate hot and cold treatment will help to reduce any swelling still remaining.

Curb

A swelling about 4in (10cm) below the hock at the back. It occurs as a result of the plantar ligament being sprained, usually due to excessive exercise, or because of poor conformation. In the initial stages of a curb forming an owner may notice heat and swelling, the horse may stand with his heel raised, and he may be or may not be lame. As soon as the owner sees the curb developing, the horse should be rested and cold treatment applied. If the horse is lame he may need an anti-inflammatory drug such as bute (phenylbutazone). A topical application which will help to reduce inflammation may also be needed, and in the long term a mild blister may stimulate the ligament to heal. However, there will always be some permanent swelling.

Splints

Bony enlargement of the splint bone, which results from strain to the ligaments. Splints usually appear on the inside of the forelegs as hard lumps, a quarter or half way down the lower leg. A horse may or may not go lame, according to the size of the splint; however, there is likely to be heat and swelling at the site, which will be painful if squeezed.

Immediately a splint is suspected the horse should be rested, whether lame or not. Cold treatment should be used as early as possible and the leg bandaged to offer some

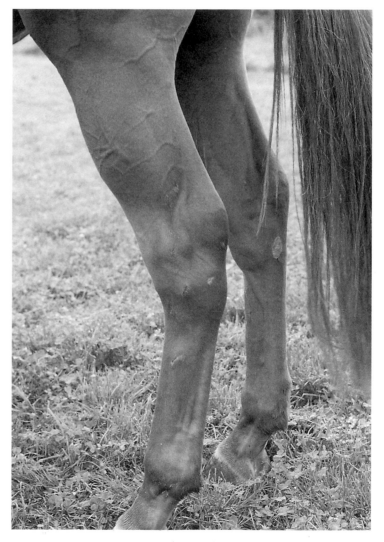

A curb just below the hock on the left hind

> **TIP**
>
> *It is sensible to try and prevent splints from occurring in the first place by avoiding working young horses on the roads too much; by wearing brushing boots for schooling and lungeing; and by ensuring that a horse's feet are attended to by the farrier regularly.*

support, (remember to bandage the other leg, too). An anti-inflammatory drug such as bute may also help to reduce inflammation. Once the initial painful stage has passed the swelling will reduce, but the horse will nearly always have a hard, permanent lump. Some splints do resolve in time and are re-absorbed; this may take a year or two, but sometimes even quite large splints will completely disappear without any treatment at all. Others, however, can cause repeated trouble throughout a horse's life.

Puffy limbs

Suffered by many horses which are stabled overnight; they usually go down with exercise and do not cause the horse any trouble. If a horse's limbs are not usually puffy, however, then the cause should be investigated further: it may be overfeeding, a blow, or possibly improper kidney function.

Tendon strain

Tendon strain occurs when the tendon has been over-stretched. Predisposing factors include fast work on hard, boggy or uneven ground; poor conformation; and faulty muscle action, perhaps as a result of fatigue.

(Left) A pronounced splint in the left fore
(Right) Tendon strain in the flexor tendon

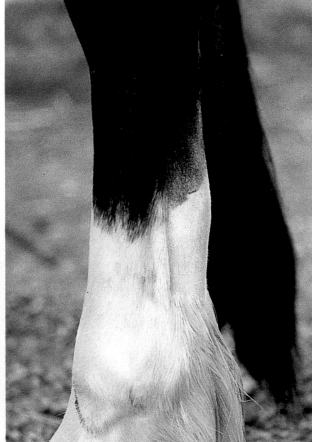

Tendon strain can be mild or very severe. In severe cases the horse will be very lame and the tendon will be hot and swollen. Touching the area will cause great pain and the horse may be unable or most unwilling to bear weight on the limb. Mild strains may be indicated by increased warmth and only very slight swelling in the leg without lameness, but such signs should be picked up quickly through routine observation, otherwise severe strain may follow.

Initial treatment is box rest and cold therapy, with ice packs and cold hosing. Pain relief in the form of anti-inflammatory drugs will be needed, and support bandaging of both limbs. The period of box rest can last for six to eight weeks, although the veterinary surgeon is the best person to advise. Short periods of in-hand walking should be introduced as soon as the acute inflammation has gone down. Long-term healing can take up to a year. However, physiotherapy can help by reducing soft tissue swelling; such treatments can include laser, ultra-sound and magnetic field therapy.

Windgalls

Pockets of fluid around the fetlock joints. Sometimes they can be pushed through from the inside of the leg to the outside. They may appear after rest and disappear with work, or vice versa, or they may be permanent. Windgalls do not usually cause lameness, and no treatment is necessary. If a horse does go lame, then further investigation is needed to establish a secondary cause.

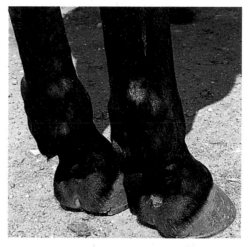

Windgalls on the hind fetlocks; these do not normally cause lameness

Thoroughpins

As windgalls, except they appear over the hocks. Any steps taken to reduce them are usually done only for cosmetic reasons, on a show horse for instance.

Capped hocks and elbows

Caused by knocks to these protruding sites. Prevention is certainly better than cure, so an owner should make sure his horse has a deep bed and a large enough box for his size. A sausage boot may help to prevent a capped elbow. Once a capped hock or elbow is established it is extremely difficult to reduce the resultant thickening. A topical application can be applied, but it is unlikely to get rid of it altogether. Physiotherapy may help if used early enough.

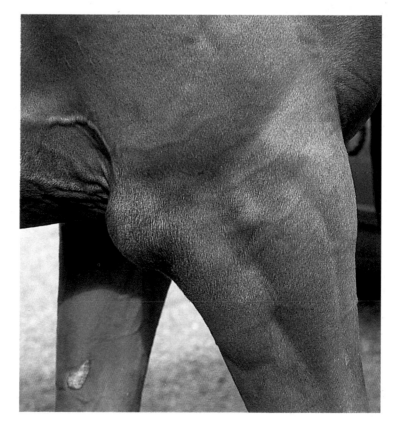

(Right) A severely capped elbow

Lymphangitis

PROBLEM Lymphangitis is not all that common, although when it occurs it can be quite worrying for a horse owner. What is it, and how is it treated?

SOLUTION Lymphangitis is a condition which is usually attributed to an infection of some sort, perhaps the result of a small injury which went undetected. An owner will notice his horse's limbs (usually, but not always, his hind limbs) start to swell from the pastern upwards; within a day they may swell up to double their normal size, which is quite alarming. The horse will probably be reluctant to move, and the owner may see a fluid seeping from the affected leg/s. He may also notice some, all, or none of these symptoms:

- a rise in temperature;
- sweating and/or trembling;
- blowing;
- lost appetite.

This is a condition which requires veterinary treatment as the horse is likely to need antibiotics and anti-inflammatory drugs. Once a horse has had lymphangitis he will be more prone to further attacks and his legs may become permanently thickened if these do occur.

The effects of lymphangitis can be quite dramatic as this photograph clearly shows

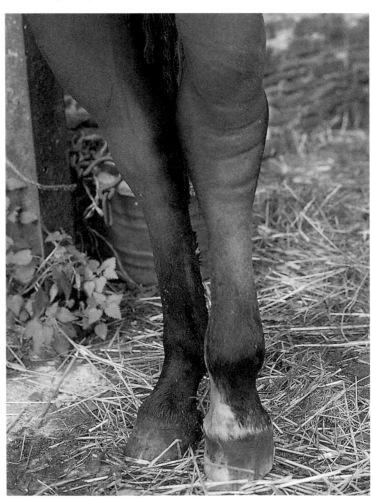

Azoturia

SOLUTION Azoturia used to be known as 'Monday morning disease' because it often occurred following a day off (usually Sunday). It is a condition where a horse's muscles go into spasm, similar to cramps as in humans. It generally affects quarters and loins.

PROBLEM What is azoturia, why was it known as Monday Morning disease, and what can be done to prevent a horse from suffering from it?

A horse may be reluctant to walk out of his box, or he may start to become stiff out on a ride, or he may suddenly stop dead and refuse to move. This is because the muscles are going into spasm and movement is extremely painful.

Immediate action

The horse should not be forced to walk home – indeed, the rider should dismount immediately and just let him stand still. He may start to sweat, so he should be kept warm with the rider's coat if nothing else is to hand. The pain may start to ease off, in which case the horse can be walked slowly back home if help cannot be summoned. Ideally, however, he should be transported home or to a nearby stable in a trailer and the vet called, particularly if the attack is bad and he is unwilling to move at all.

Once a horse has had an azoturia attack, he will be more susceptible to it in the future. Essentially this condition results from the accumulation of glycogen in the blood – usually because of a diet too rich in carbohydrate for the horse's workload – which when it is used up results in a marked increase in the production of lactic acid; it is this overload which causes swelling and damage to the muscle fibres. The actual cause is not fully understood, although it can be appreciated that it is very important to observe a strict feeding and exercise pattern. Once a vet has carried out tests on a horse with azoturia he will advise the owner as to how to proceed.

A horse with azoturia will not want to walk out of his box; any movement at all will hurt him

Managing arthritis

PROBLEM What exactly is arthritis, why do many horses suffer from it, especially older ones, and what hope is there for the horse in the long term?

SOLUTION Arthritis means inflammation of a joint, and any of the joints in the body can be affected, especially if they have had their fair share of work over the years; this is why the condition appears more frequently in older competition and hunting horses. The affected joints are often warm and swollen, which causes pain.

Immediate action

The only way to be sure that a horse has arthritis is to have a vet X-ray the problem site. If arthritis is diagnosed, then treatment involves good management, rather than a cure. Initially the horse will find relief from cold hosing and rest, but in the long term an owner must look towards managing the condition by relieving the pain with anti-inflammatory drugs. There are other treatments available which are aimed at helping a horse to remain in work, and scientific research is developing new treatments all the time, so the vet should be asked about these.

Colic

PROBLEM Finding a horse lying down, rolling or kicking in pain, can be very distressing, but it is a situation where an owner must keep calm and try to discover the cause as quickly as possible. What is the most likely cause, and what immediate action should be taken?

SOLUTION If an owner discovers his horse acting oddly in the stable or field, a prime suspect for the cause is colic: this is abdominal pain which comes from the digestive system, or in the case of renal colic, from the kidneys, and it can vary from a mild attack to an extremely painful and distressing one.

A horse with colic may be standing or lying down. He will be generally uneasy, possibly sweating, and will often look towards his stomach and perhaps try to kick at it with his hind legs. He may paw the ground, rub his tail or box walk in an attempt to relieve the discomfort. Many horses with colic will get down and up frequently, and some will roll violently. By doing so they are capable of twisting their intestines, referred to as a 'twisted gut', and the consequences can be fatal.

A horse with colic may frequently attempt to urinate, but may only be able to pass small amounts or even none at all. He may also attempt to pass droppings but finds he is incapable of doing so, or only passes small amounts and/or large quantities of wind.

Immediate action

If an owner suspects his horse has colic, he should take his temperature – it does not usually rise above normal. Next, he should check his pulse, which will rise in relation to the amount of pain he is experiencing. He should *not* be given a colic drench, or any-

---

Horses seem to be more susceptible to colic than other animals and most cases of colic can be attributed to one (or more, though this is unlikely) of the following:
- *worm infestation, where the horse has not been given regular worming treatment, or the appropriate type for a particular problem;*
- *irregular feeding;*
- *drinking large quantities of cold water while the horse is still hot;*
- *sudden changes of diet;*
- *poor quality food;*
- *incomplete mastication of food due to poor teeth;*
- *anxiety or stress.*

A horse with colic may attempt to roll violently: this may induce a 'twisted gut', which can be fatal

thing to eat. If he is lying down but not rolling he should *not* be forced to get up, as this is his way of dealing with the pain. If he is restless in the box, he should be put in a bridle and walked around for five or ten minutes on a soft surface – the paddock or a sand school, for example. However, if the owner finds that the horse keeps trying to throw himself to the ground, it will be safer to keep him in his box with a deep bed if possible, or to let him loose in an enclosed school, rather than risk injury.

If a horse seems to be finding relief quickly, then the owner should stay with him and monitor his progress: thus if he starts to urinate or pass droppings freely, or stops getting down and up, and ceases to look round at his stomach or to paw the ground, then these are all good signs that the pain is decreasing.

When to call the vet

Most cases of colic are not serious, so an owner need not always call the vet. However, if a horse does not start to improve quickly, then it is better to call the vet sooner rather than later, as there is no way of knowing if it is serious or not. An owner should always call the vet, stating it is an emergency, if the horse:

■ has a pulse rate exceeding 45–50;

■ has eye membranes deeper than a salmon pink (although the owner should bear in mind what is normal for that particular horse);

Some owners prefer to walk a colicky horse around on a soft surface while waiting for the vet to arrive

- does not find any relief from what appears to be a mild attack, within half-an-hour;
- is obviously distressed or violent;
- is rolling violently;
- is attempting to pass urine or droppings, but cannot.

Frequently, all that is needed is a painkiller administered by the vet to prevent the horse from injuring himself until the whole episode passes. However, once the vet arrives he will be able to examine the horse fully and take whatever further action is necessary. He will find it useful if the owner can tell him whether:

- the horse has passed any droppings. The owner should take a note of the time if he has, and keep them for the vet to examine;
- the horse's stomach has been making any funny sounds – if so, what were they like?
- the horse's diet has been changed, or he has been turned out onto grass for the first time in a while;
- the horse is in constant pain, or only seems to be in pain intermittently.

Diarrhoea

CAUSE
There are various causes of diarrhoea:
- A change in diet (this will be known to the owner).
- Excitement (this will be known to the owner).
- Nervousness (may be evident, but the owner may not know why).
- Worms – when was the horse last wormed?
- Administration of antibiotics by a vet for another condition.
- An infection – an owner will have no way of knowing without an examination by a vet.
- Poisioning – are there any poisonous plants in the field? Have stables or fences been recently treated? Have there been any strangers around who might have given the horse something?

SOLUTION
If the cause of the diarrhoea is known – for example, the horse always get excited when at shows and develops diarrhoea, or he has suddenly been turned out onto lush grass – then there is no need to be alarmed.

Treatment of diarrhoea should be methodical:
- Firstly, put the horse in his stable.
- Provide good quality hay and plenty of fresh, clean water.
- Do not feed succulents (apples or carrots for example) or sugar beet.
- Electrolytes can be added to the horse's water, but it is important to be sure that he will drink them happily before leaving him. It is more important that he drinks water, so electrolytes should be avoided if he obviously dislikes their taste.
- Gradually the horse can be reintroduced to grass, if this was the cause of the diarrhoea, although his grazing should be limited to short periods at a time.
- If the cause of the condition is not known, then the vet should be called, because the diarrhoea may be a symptom of another condition.

PROBLEM
Diarrhoea can be mild, in which case it usually clears up without complications; or it can be severe, in which case veterinary intervention is necessary. How can an owner judge the severity of the condition, and what action can he take?

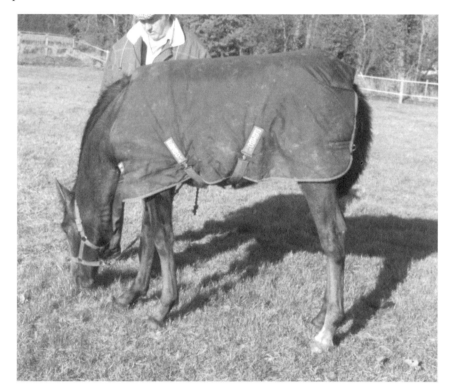

If too much rich grass has caused your horse's diarrhoea, you can introduce it gradually back into his diet, under controlled conditions, once he has improved

Electrolytes can be added to the horse's water, but it is important to ensure he is quite happy to drink water containing them

Mucking about in mud

PROBLEM Mud fever, rainscald and cracked heels are all skin complaints that can affect a horse in the winter months. What causes them and how are they treated?

SOLUTION These conditions are caused by a dermatitis bacterium (*dermatophilus congolensis*) which thrives in damp, muddy conditions and produces scabby, eczema-like symptoms which can be very painful. The condition is known as mud fever when the legs are affected, rainscald when the back is affected, and cracked heels when symptoms are shown in the hollows of the pasterns.

Extreme vigilance is needed where a horse is susceptible to these skin conditions, because not only are they painful, they can also lead to more serious infections. For example, if mud fever is left untreated, it can spread up the legs to the flexor tendons and cause serious lameness.

These complaints commonly affect horses that are turned out into wet, muddy paddocks. Prolonged soaking softens the skin, enabling the bacterium to enter, and the abrasive action of mud breaks the skin which then makes entry even easier. The bacterium which causes mud fever forms spores which are capable of surviving on the horse's coat for months, if not years. It can therefore flare up at any time, and horses have been known to show symptoms of mud fever in the middle of summer.

Action to take

Mud fever is recognised by scabby lesions which can become inflamed and very painful. If the horse has white legs he will be more susceptible, and the pasterns are commonly affected.

Cracked heels start as scurf and scabs in the hollow at the back of the pastern, and these develop into painful cracks. It is therefore important to keep a close eye on the horse and to check him every day when he is brought in for grooming. If his legs need to be hosed off, they should be dried gently but thoroughly afterwards. If the mud is dry, it is better to brush it off, but *gently* – vigorous brushing with coarse bristles can cause more of the abrasions which allow the mud fever bacterium to enter.

Treatment should begin at the very first sign of infection. The first thing to do is to eliminate the cause, so the horse should be taken off the paddock and stabled. Any long hair around the affected area should

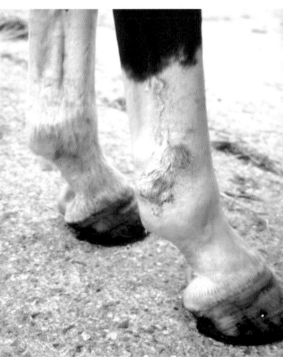

then be clipped away and the scabs gently removed to expose the condition to the air. The scabs will be hard and crusty, and their removal may be extremely painful for the horse: to minimise the pain, they should first be moistened by washing with an antibacterial soap and warm water. If the condition has been neglected, the scabs may need to be soaked for at least half an hour before trying to remove them. This can be done by simply hosing them; or by using a hose boot; or by tubbing with warm water.

Once the scabs have been removed the area will look very sore. It should be dried thoroughly by gently patting with clean gamgee, and a soothing antibiotic ointment such as Dermobion then applied twice daily. Dermobion is a green ointment that contains corticosteriod; it therefore helps to reduce any inflammation, which may be a factor in more severe cases of the condition. If the bedding is likely to stick to the sore areas then a stable bandage should be put on over a clean layer of gamgee. If possible, however, the horse should be allowed to stand unbandaged in a stable without bedding – rubber matting is ideal.

After a few days of such treatment the condition should be drying up nicely, with new hair already starting to grow. More severe cases may need poulticing before the scabs are removed, as secondary bacterial infection often develops, requiring a course of antibiotics. The warm poultice should be squeezed out as much as possible before it is applied, as it will then draw out the infection and any remaining dirt. The warmth will also help to increase the blood supply to the damaged area, and this will promote healing and reduce inflammation. Once the poultice is removed, the condition can be treated as before. Where a secondary bacterial infection has developed, a course of antibiotics may be needed.

> **TIP**
>
> As with many complaints, the prevention of mud fever and its associated conditions is better than cure. In the winter months a field gateway can turn into a quagmire: it is a good idea to put shale down in front of gates and water troughs or wherever else horses congregate, so they don't stand for long periods in sloppy mud.
>
> Keeping a horse dry and clean is of course the best of all, but where this is not possible, a barrier cream such as zinc and castor oil or liquid paraffin may be applied to protect susceptible areas such as heels and pasterns. If this is put on before the horse is turned out in muddy conditions it will help to prevent the disease from breaking out.

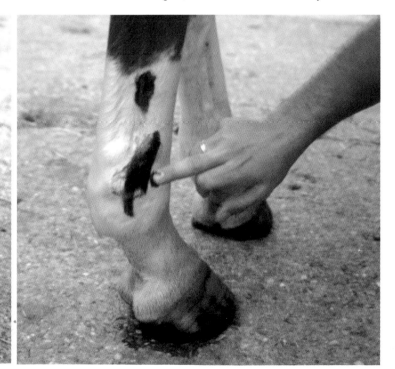

Mud fever: *(Far left) Soak the affected area with warm water to soften and so aid the removal of the crusty scabs*

(Centre left) Once the scabs have been removed the area will look and feel very sore

(Left) Dermobion, a green ointment containing corticosteroid, or a similar application recommended by your veterinary surgeon, should then be applied to aid healing

Sweet itch

PROBLEM   Sweet itch is a skin condition which causes horses to rub their manes and tails; it is a reaction to the saliva of the culicoid midge which is active during the months from April to November. The severity of the condition varies from horse to horse: some will only rub occasionally, while others will rub themselves bald, causing open sores. What can an owner do if his horse is susceptible?

SOLUTION   Sweet itch is a condition which should be carefully managed, rather than waiting for it to occur and then treating it. The midges that cause the trouble are more active around dusk and again around dawn, and if possible the owner should make sure the horse is stabled at these times. If this is not possible there are precautions that can be taken.

An owner can:
- put a summer sheet on the horse while he is out in the field, making sure it is secure;
- use a linen hood, which covers half the head and the mane, and a linen tail guard, from 3.30pm to 8.30am;
- feed the horse garlic;

A horse with sweet itch will often rub his mane, tail, hips and even belly, to the point of being extremely sore

After washing the horse a soothing lotion such as benzyl benzoate, or a midge repellent ointment such as Camrosa, should be applied to discourage the midges from biting the affected areas

- keep the horse away from grazing areas which have ponds in the vicinity;
- use a long-acting fly repellent.

Action to take

If a horse develops sweet itch, an owner should begin to treat it immediately. A good shampoo should be obtained from the vet, preferably a spray-on kind which works its way right into the hair; this should be rubbed well in to help remove any scurf and scabs. Be careful to rinse it out well, or else the horse might start rubbing as a result of shampoo irritation. This should be repeated every week while the horse suffers from the condition, and after washing, a soothing lotion such as benzyl benzoate should be rubbed in twice a day as this will also help to discourage the midges from biting and will give the horse some relief. Make sure it is rubbed well into all areas, including the underside of the mane, tail and belly.

Putting a summer sheet on the horse while out in the field will also help to deter midges from biting

Ringworm

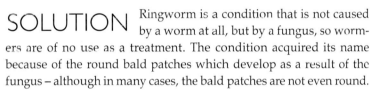

PROBLEM What sort of worm causes ringworm, and can it be cleared up by the use of wormers?

SOLUTION Ringworm is a condition that is not caused by a worm at all, but by a fungus, so wormers are of no use as a treatment. The condition acquired its name because of the round bald patches which develop as a result of the fungus – although in many cases, the bald patches are not even round.

There is little that can be done to prevent ringworm, as it is very contagious and has a long incubation period; thus a horse could have come into contact with a contagious horse three months earlier, and be only just developing the condition. As soon as an owner realises that his horse has ringworm, he must isolate him. The condition is treated by using a topical antibiotic skin wash, all over the horse. This is usually done three times at three-day intervals, and then again two weeks later if necessary. If the condition is established, treat with Griseofulvin (although this must not be used for brood mares), an antifungal antibiotic which is put in a horse's feed for seven to ten days. Ensure strict standards of hygiene by disinfecting all tack and stables with a fungicidal solution, and do not touch other horses without first disinfecting the hands and clothes.

An early indication of ringworm infection reveals itself as slight 'tufts' of hair on the coat, which soon develop into raised blotches of hair which will fall off easily and which continue to do so until small hairless patches of crusty skin are seen, which may or may not exude a small amount of serum. They commonly appear around the girth and saddle areas, or anywhere where tack meets the skin, but they will often spread all over the body.

Often the typical type of 'ring' appears and spreads all over the horse's coat. Once a stage has been reached where the patches are dry and scaly, it will take about four weeks for the hair to regrow. Coconut oil can be used to encourage the hair to grow back strong and the right colour.

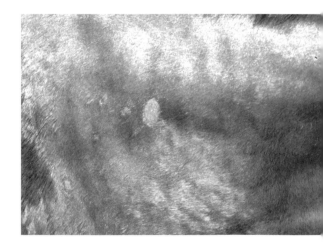

Hairless patches of crusty skin – the classic signs of ringworm

Tack injuries

PROBLEM What are the most common sites for tack injuries to appear, why do they develop, and what treatment should be carried out to remedy them?

SOLUTION A sore which develops as a result of the girth or saddle rubbing is called a 'gall'; it is a thickening of the skin caused by constant rubbing and uneven pressure. The most common sites for saddle sores are the withers, the middle of the back along the spine and sometimes they also appear on either side of the back where the saddle panels cause constant friction points.

Girth galls

Girth galls can develop as a result of a soft, flabby horse wearing a tough leather girth; or because the girth constantly rubs back and forth while in use; or because it is too wide to sit comfortably in the horse's sternum curve.

A string girth can be useful in securing a saddle which slips when using a plain leather girth. However, if they are not fitted carefully they can pinch the skin between the strands and if they are pulled up tightly from one side only, they will wrinkle the skin underneath, which leads to discomfort and sores. To ensure this does not happen, a horse's forelegs should always be pulled forwards after saddling to make certain the skin is lying flat underneath.

An Atherstone girth is shaped behind the shoulder to prevent the problem of pinching, nevertheless measures should be taken to ensure the skin is lying flat. If a horse is likely to develop a girth gall, perhaps because he has just been brought back into work and is still flabby, then preventative measures should be taken. A soft cotton girth, rather than a tougher leather one should be used, for example, or a sheepskin girth sleeve which slips over the girth to provide a soft cushion between tack and skin can be employed. To harden a horse's skin, surgical spirit or salt water can be rubbed daily into the areas most prone to galling.

A string girth pinching the skin

A girth gall: these can easily be avoided if owners follow the basics of saddle care and fitting

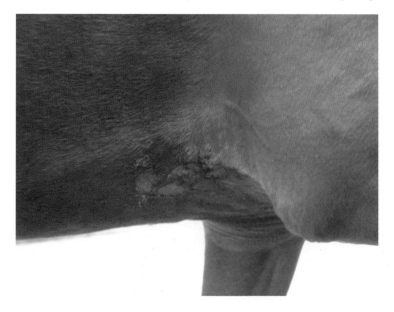

Saddle sores

Ill-fitting saddles can be very painful for the horse, and no horse should be expected to put up with such discomfort. In mild cases the horse may develop back pain, and in more severe cases he may develop nasty sores where the saddle has been constantly rubbing back and forth. To prevent such injuries a qualified saddler should always fit a new saddle to a horse and the owner should continually reassess the situation, as horses change shape according to the work that they are doing. In many cases the saddle can be reflocked to ensure a correct fit, but if the saddle cannot be 'set up' to fit exactly, or if an owner changes his horse and the saddle cannot be adapted to his shape, then it will have to be changed.

It is easy to tell if a horse has had a saddle sore, as the hair usually grows back white at the site of injury. To try and encourage the horse's normal coat colour to grow back, coconut oil can be rubbed in three times daily as soon as the sore develops.

Fitting a saddle

When fitting a saddle, ensure that when viewed from behind, daylight can be seen through to the pommel, and that four fingers (three if mounted) can be placed between the horse's withers and the pommel. Also check that the saddle doesn't pinch a horse on either side of his withers, behind the shoulders. To make sure of a good fit, always carry out such tests both dismounted and mounted.

If a numnah or shock-absorbing foam is used under the saddle it should be pulled well up into the gullet of the saddle or it will slip down, put pressure on the spine and possibly cause sores. Badly chosen and poorly fitted numnahs can have the adverse effect of overheating a horse's back and wrinkling, which is a common cause of sores. In addition, if the saddle is just on the borderline of being too tight, then a numnah will make it tighter.

White areas around the saddle area confirm previous saddle sores

---

TIP

Prevention is always better than cure, and most tack-related sores can be prevented. First, an owner should make sure the horse's tack fits him properly – if in doubt, he should ask a good saddler or an experienced instructor. Then he should ensure that his horse is always clean underneath his tack, which should be kept clean and supple, and he should always check his horse's tack once it is fitted on the horse.

A saddle cloth or numnah should be pulled well up into the gullet of the saddle otherwise it will pull tight over the withers and cause pressure on the spine, which may lead to sores

Flu

PROBLEM Just like their owners, horses can suffer from 'flu. What are the signs to look out for, and how is a horse with 'flu best managed?

SOLUTION A horse with 'flu will generally feel as his owner might – very tired and irritable, and generally unwell. If an owner suspects his horse may have 'flu, he should isolate him immediately, examine him closely and call for the vet. He should look for:

- a raised temperature, which might be anything from between 101.5–106 °F (38.6–41.1°C);
- a loss of appetite;
- a dry, rasping cough;
- a watery discharge, or if the horse has been suffering for some days, a thicker discoloured discharge may be observed;
- glands which are enlarged. These can be observed between the horse's upper cheek bones and neck, and under the lower jaw;
- watery or weeping eyes;
- shivering.

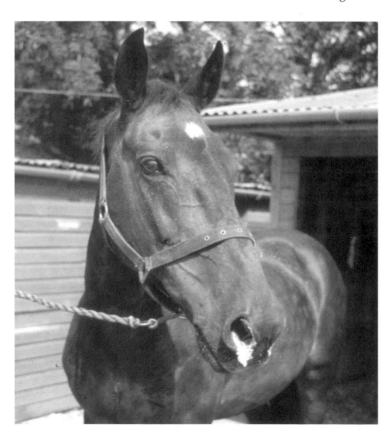

A horse who has suffered from 'flu for a few days may develop a thick, discoloured discharge from the nostrils

Action to take

If a horse does have 'flu he will need to be kept warm with rugs and stable bandages, in a stable with a good deep bed; draughts should be prevented, but it should be very well ventilated.

If the horse seems to have difficulty in swallowing he may have a sore throat, and placing warm cloths over his glands and throat will give him some relief. An owner should always make sure he has plenty of fresh clean water, although this should not be too cold.

To treat any nasal discharge, a steaming cloth can be put in the bottom of a muzzle (the leather type which is not totally enclosed; an enclosed fibreglass one will restrict his breathing if a cloth is placed in the bottom), onto which a few drops of eucalyptus or Friar's balsam can be put; this will also help to loosen any congestion. Failing a muzzle, a small hessian sack can be tied on to a headcollar and the steaming cloth can be placed into this. The owner must make sure the cloth is not so hot that it will scald the horse's nose if he reaches down and touches it. He should not be left unattended while using steam inhalation.

Once a horse's temperature has gone down he will benefit from being turned out, although he will still need to be kept warm. Once all the symptoms have disappeared, the owner should give him a further two weeks' rest before bringing him back into light work.

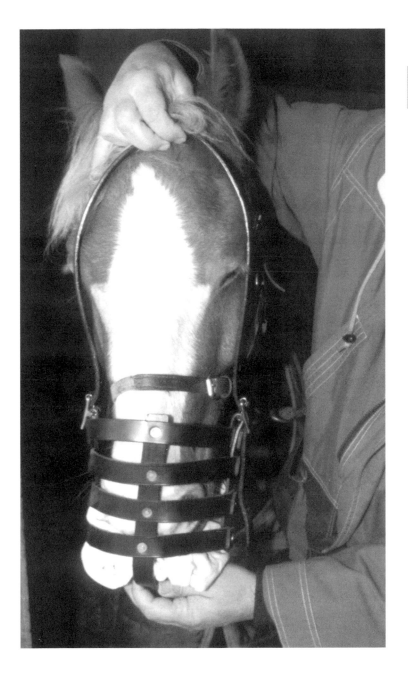

A steaming cloth with a few drops of eucalyptus or Friar's balsam on it will help to loosen any congestion

---

TIP

It is very important that all horses living together, whether in the field or within the stable yard, are vaccinated regularly. It is also irresponsible to take an unvaccinated horse to a competition, as he may carry the infection and pass it on. This is why most shows now insist on seeing a current certificate of vaccination. If all owners act responsibly and have all their horses vaccinated, then far fewer horses will ever suffer from this infectious disease.

Viruses

PROBLEM The biggest worry to competitors is that their horse may get 'the virus' and lose form. In fact, horses suffer from many viral infections which usually cause symptoms similar to mild equine influenza. How can an owner detect a virus, and what can be done about it?

SOLUTION Horses with a virus may appear listless and less willing to do as requested. They often have a runny nose, ranging from a watery discharge to a thick, purulent discharge. Horses with a virus may or may not cough.

The most common virus to affect horses is equine herpes virus type 1 (EHV1), which is spread easily from horse to horse. Unlike 'flu there is no effective vaccine, and treatment is usually complete rest until the horse recovers; sufferers have been known to take up to three months to regain their former condition.

The final decision

PROBLEM

No owner wants to think about the time when his horse may no longer be around , but if the horse is getting very old or is constantly ill, then decisions have to be made. What are the options when having a horse put down, and what might help an owner to decide one way or the other?

Many horses can enjoy a good quality of life into advanced old age; it is up to every owner to ensure that their horse does not suffer on account of their being unable to 'let go'

SOLUTION

The most satisfactory end is where an old horse gently slips away in his paddock. Although losing him will never be easy, it does help if an owner knows that he has had a good life and has died peacefully. More traumatic is having to decide whether it is fair to keep a horse alive with the quality of life that he has. Deciding to put a horse down is called euthanasia. Making the decision is never easy, but letting a horse suffer because an owner cannot face up to the fact that it is best to let him go, is unkind. The biggest factor in making the right decision is evaluating his quality of life, and to quantify this you shoud ask:

- is he in pain?
- is he constantly on drugs to relieve the pain?
- is his condition likely to improve, or will it get progressively worse?
- is he old and very stiff?
- does he find walking difficult?
- does he find eating difficult?
- does he keep suffering from one complaint after another?
- if he has to be sold is he going to a kind, caring home?

While a vet will advise whether euthanasia is the kindest option if a horse is suffering from an illness, especially if he is in pain, only his owner will know whether it is time to let him go gracefully if he is simply getting old. It is an extremely difficult decision to make, but it is often kinder to have a horse put down at home, than to pass him on to another home where he might be abused.

Horses should only be destroyed by a qualified vet or knacker-man. There are two main ways of putting a horse down: by shooting with a humane killer, or by injecting with a lethal dose of drugs, and the owner should have some idea of what to expect.

The humane killer is cheaper, is relatively quick and is very efficient, but the owner will witness his horse dropping to the ground like a stone, and grunting as the air is forced from the lungs. The animal's body will then twitch for a few minutes. The whole process is noiser and, of course, messier.

A lethal injection will cost more, but is generally a calmer and cleaner method; some horses, however, dislike injections intensely and will fight against the effects of the drug until it overpowers them (rather like a wild animal that has been darted to sedate it) and they 'go to sleep'.

Having a horse put down can be a heart-rending decision, but it is the owner's ultimate responsibility to his horse.

FEEDING

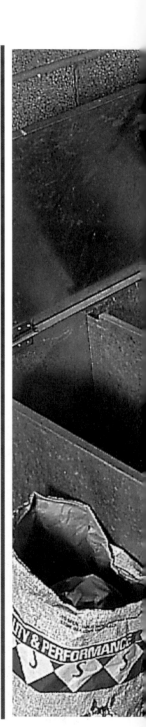

Part 4:
& NUTRITION

Worries about weight

PROBLEM When discussing feed quantities, most people talk in terms of scoops. What measurement is a scoop, and how does this relate to the weight of a given foodstuff?

SOLUTION A scoop is not a measure at all, it is simply a piece of equipment used to transfer a horse's feed to his feeding trough; moreover there are many designs of feed scoop, and each will hold a different quantity of each feed type. Feed should be measured in terms of pounds or kilograms. In order to find out how much a scoop holds in weight, rather than quantity, it is necessary to put the scoop on a set of kitchen scales and then set the scales to zero, and a scoop of each feed type can then be weighed accurately. Even in the case of 'complete feeds' it is still essential to feed by weight, and so you need to know how much a certain scoop holds. For instance, if a scoop holds 2lb (900g) of coarse mix and a horse requires 2.5lb (1.1kg) of feed a day, it is easy to work out that he needs one and a quarter scoops of feed. As a rough guide, a round plastic scoop (as illustrated) usually holds about:

- 1lb (450g) of chaff;
- 2lb (900g) of coarse mix;
- 3lb (1.3kg) of nuts.

A scoop of nuts weighs far more heavily than a scoop of chaff and yet a scoop of chaff appears to go a very long way, so it is important to feed by 'weight', not volume

Feeding and exercise

SOLUTION To start with, an owner needs to work out how much feed his horse should be receiving for the work he is doing. This is not as simple as is sounds because each horse is an individual, so it is impossible to lay down firm guidelines. Feeding too little will result in poor condition and loss of energy, while feeding too much will cause a horse to develop conditions such as azoturia (see page 113), as well as making him dangerously obese and badly behaved.

The first step in working out how much to feed is to determine a horse's bodyweight. If access can be gained to a weighbridge (look in the local directory for public weighbridges) an owner can find out exactly how much his horse weighs (though he should remember to take his own weight into consideration if he is holding him). Otherwise a special weighing tape for horses, or an ordinary tape measure can be used. To determine a horse's weight an owner will need to take two measurements:

PROBLEM How can an owner judge whether or not his horse is being fed and exercised properly?

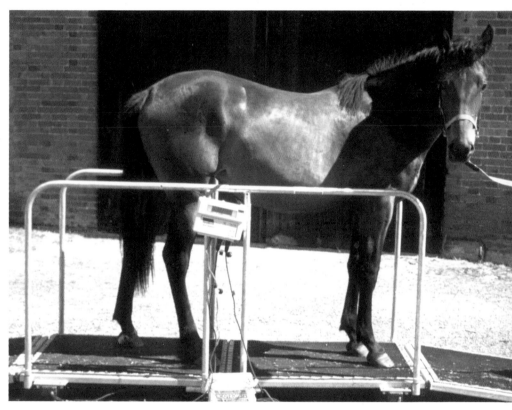

A weighbridge always provides a very accurate measurement of a horse's weight

- the heart girth, which is a measurement taken around the horse just behind the withers;
- the length from the point of buttocks to the point of shoulder.

These two measurements are then put into the following equation to find out a horse's bodyweight in pounds:

Bodyweight (lb) = heart girth (in)^2 x length (in) divided by 241.3

Having determined this figure, an owner can then begin to work out how much to feed his horse in relation to the work he is doing with him. The average horse should receive about 2.5 per cent of his bodyweight in feed per day. Having established this, an owner then needs to decide upon a suitable ratio of roughage (forage such as hay or haylage) to concentrates ('hard feeds' such as coarse mixes, cubes and oats) for his workload.

Inevitably an owner will find that he is continually assessing his horse's condition, and so also his diet.

Overfeeding

PROBLEM

It is now recognised that overfeeding horses is extremely common. Why is this, what effects can overfeeding have on horses, and how can owners be re-educated to feed less?

TIP

Every horse owner's rule should be 'Feed as little as possible for the amount of work done or the condition to be maintained'.

This horse could do with losing a little weight to improve his overall condition

SOLUTION

Overfeeding is a common malpractice because owners want to feel that they are providing the horse with everything he needs – they want to be good owners! However, overfeeding is a temptation that should be resisted if the horse is to feel fit and healthy.

Most owners feel that as soon as a horse does more work and starts to get fitter, he must have more feed. While to a certain extent this is true, fitter horses will benefit from being leaner, so a horse who is already quite round may not require any more feed at all. A horse carrying a fair amount of weight will feel more lethargic and will therefore struggle when asked to exert himself, and so will be unable to perform to his optimum ability.

Any advice given on feeding is inevitably generalised, because it is such a complex subject. Every owner needs to know his own horse really well before he can hope to establish a feeding regime that suits him perfectly.

Horses who are overfed are also likely to suffer from nutritional problems, research having shown that over 90 per cent of nutritionally related diseases come from overfeeding, with less than 5 per cent from underfeeding. For example, azoturia is a common problem in fit competition horses who are overfed: feeding too much results in a slow and steady build-up of glycogen in the muscles (the method by which the horse's body stores energy); when these muscles are required to work, this glycogen breaks down and lactic acid is produced. If too much lactic acid is produced, however, the muscle structure can break down, and this can be extremely dangerous to the horse.

While too much feed may not be the direct cause, overweight horses can be more susceptible to a number of conditions such as:

- colic;
- laminitis;
- sweet itch;
- skin allergies;
- joint problems;
- respiratory disease.

Just as too much fat puts a strain on the horse's joints, it can also increase the workload of the internal organs such as the heart and the liver.

Physical appearance

SOLUTION An owner should make a point of assessing his horse's condition every month, because if he is with the horse day in, day out, small changes may be occurring which he might not notice. He should take his horse's measurements to determine any change if he is unsure, and should do something about it if the horse starts to lose or to gain weight.

PROBLEM The best indication of whether an owner is successfully providing his horse with a good, balanced feeding and fitness programme is his horse's appearance: in short, he should be guided by his condition, and once he has found a routine that works, he should not be tempted to fiddle around with it. However, it is often said that if you see a horse all day, every day, you fail to notice small differences until they become obvious. So how can an owner assess his horse's condition without becoming complacent?

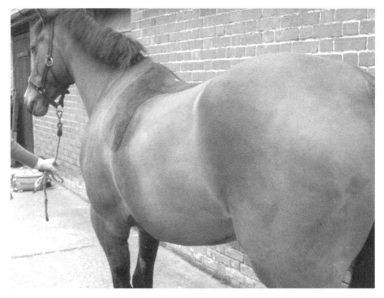

When assessing a horse's condition view him at an angle from behind

Viewing a horse from the side can be deceptive because a fairly 'flat' picture is obtained; it is more useful to view him at an angle from behind. A horse should be well covered, with no ribs sticking out, and he should be generally nice and round without being obese.

Special considerations

■ A fat horse is not a healthy horse. His heart and joints will be under stress, particularly when worked. It is wise to follow a programme of controlled exercise and diet until a horse loses weight and becomes fitter, when he can resume his normal training programme.

■ A 'good doer', as long as he is being reasonably fed, always manages to maintain his good condition whatever his workload.

■ Horses with less-than-perfect conformation are often more difficult to keep in good condition.

■ Youngsters need to be fed carefully: they need enough food to maintain healthy growth, but they must not become too fat because this would put unnecessary strain on their growing joints.

■ It is far more difficult to keep an older horse in good condition, and the question of whether to retire him or not usually arises at some point. As long as he is in no pain and still enjoys his work, there is no need to do so – indeed, many working horses decline far more rapidly if retired.

Feed me now!

PROBLEM Some horses have a poor appetite, while others seem to want feeding constantly. What can be done to satisfy a horse who always seems hungry?

SOLUTION It is important that the horse's owner establishes why he always seems hungry: is it that he is not receiving enough food, or is he just plain greedy? First the horse's condition should be assessed: if rather on the thin side, then obviously he is not getting enough to eat; if he is well covered he may just have a fast metabolism (this means that his body gets through whatever is eaten rather quickly). Eating quite a lot of hay can be normal in certain situations – in fact, if the grazing on offer is sparse, then it is not unusual for a horse to eat half to three-quarters of a bale of hay overnight when stabled (an average bale weighs 50lbs/23kg). Surprisingly, lush grass may not see that much of a reduction in the amount of hay consumed overnight because grass contains a high proportion of water, so the horse will want to make up his fibre intake with hay, given the opportunity. Other causes of a horse being ravenous may include:

■ Worms – a veterinary surgeon can take a blood and dung sample to ensure a horse is worm-free.

■ Tooth problems – sharp teeth may prevent the horse from masticating his feed properly, which means that whole grains may simply be passing straight through his digestive tract. A vet or tooth specialist should advise on this.

■ A highly strung temperament – if a horse is by nature anxious, he may simply be 'worrying' the weight off. Any calming measures, such as calming herbs or a change of environment, should be considered.

■ The wrong type of feed being given – low energy feeds may simply not be enough for the horse, so these should be changed for higher energy ones: from ordinary horse and pony cubes or mix, to competition cubes or mix for example. Such feeds have a higher protein and energy content as well as containing more vitamins and minerals so they should sustain a horse for longer periods.

Down to basics

PROBLEM What are the horse's basic dietary needs, and what is the best way of providing them?

SOLUTION The horse's first dietary need is water, and it must be available to him all day, every day so that he can drink when he wants. The other essential dietary needs are:

■ carbohydrates – for energy;
■ protein – for growth and repair;
■ fibre – to maintain the horse's digestive system in good order;
■ fats – for warmth;
■ vitamins and minerals – for correct bodily function.

In an ideal world, good grass and herbage during the spring and summer would provide the horse with sufficient levels of all these nutrients to sustain him in good health all the year round. However, as a horse no longer lives in an ideal world – in that he is confined to a stable or small paddock and is obliged to use up energy every time he is ridden or driven – the available grass will almost certainly need to be supplemented. Thus in winter he will need hay to help him maintain the minimum levels of required nutrients, and when he is worked he will need extra energy in the form of high energy carbohydrates.

How much of a horse's total feed ration is made up of roughage, and how much concentrates, depends on his weight and the amount and type of work being carried out. An approximate guide is:

Type of Work	Hay (as percentage)	Concentrates (as percentage)
Maintenance	100%	0%
Light work (slow, short hacks)	80-100%	0-20%
Medium work (normal hacking, schooling, riding club activities)	60-80%	20-40%
Hard work (in training for competitions, competitions, eventing, intensive schooling)	40 50%	60-60%
Ultra fitness (racing, three-day eventing)	25%	75%

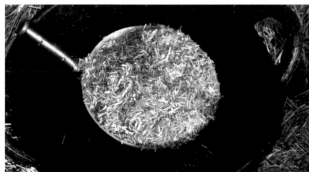

Chaff provides roughage and stops a horse from bolting his food

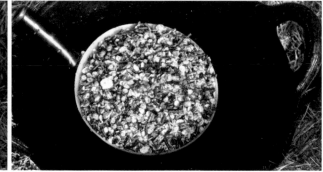

Coarse mix nutritionally balanced, convenient and easy to feed

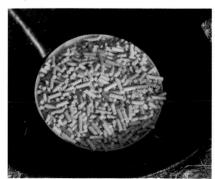

Maize is a high-energy feed which is low in protein and deficient in fibre

Supplements: these form part of the nutritional content of a feed

Sugar beet pulp: provides 'slow-release' energy

Grass roots

PROBLEM When there is little rainfall grass is said to be of poorer quality, even if there is still a plentiful supply. Why is this?

SOLUTION Just as a horse needs to drink water in order to survive, so does grass, and during the heat of the day grass can quite often be seen starting to turn brown and dry. Paddocks will 'burn off' completely if they are relatively exposed and there has been no rainfall for some time. Without adequate rain, grass develops a high ratio of stem to leaf, and this is of poorer nutritional quality than grass with a plentiful supply of leaf. Stemmy grass is of poor protein content and is also more difficult to digest. Sparse rainfall also results in less clover, leading to further reduction in the protein levels of the pasture. What this means is that even though there appears to be a lot of long grass, the horse may not be able to gain enough nutrition from it for maintenance. Horses who are growing, working or lactating may therefore need to be fed a protein supplement during such times.

Hydroponics

PROBLEM Hydroponic grass is an artificially grown source used to feed many horses which have access to little or no pasture. What are the advantages and disadvantages of such grass, and how practical would it be for the average owner to feed his horse hydroponically grown grass?

SOLUTION Hydroponic machines grow seeds that produce grass in a soil-less environment in trays under controlled conditions. Most machines are heated and have a light source to enable the grass to turn green. Units are available in different sizes, from the two horse up to the many horse size, producing between 45 and 2,200lb (20–1,000kg) of fresh grass per day. The advantages of hydroponics include:

- Forage 'on tap'. Where horses cannot be turned out they can benefit from eating grass of a stable nutritional quality all year round.
- Ideal as a hay replacer for horses with dust allergies.
- Early breeding as the availability of fresh green forage may stimulate mares to come in to season.
- Fussy feeders may be more tempted to eat fresh grass than hay.
- Prevention of fields becoming poached in really wet weather, as forage can be offered in the stable or barn.

The disadvantages include:

- High initial outlay, although hire purchase agreements available.
- The grass contains a low quantity of dry matter.
- The seeds (barley) from which the grass is grown are low in calcium and high in phosphorous so a supplementary calcium source (such as alfalfa) will be a necessary addition to the horse's diet.
- Energy values are low, so horses in work, lactating or growing will require supplementary feeding.

Only the individual owner can decide whether the advantages outweigh the disadvantages. However, since hydroponically grown grass is unlikely to fulfil either the total nutritional requirements of the horse, or his psychological requirements, as he should still be turned out to exercise and allowed to unwind, the individual owner is unlikely to find that the convenience of such a unit outweighs the financial costs.

Hydroponic grass unit showing various stages of growth

The importance of forage

SOLUTION Hay is generally available as meadow hay or seed hay. Meadow hay is taken from a permanent pasture and is finer and softer than seed hay, which as its name implies is a hay of grass grown as seed the year before. Meadow hay is said to be more suitable for ponies and roughed-off horses, and seed hay for horses in fast work – hunters, eventers, racehorses – because it is higher in protein; this also applies to lucerne and alfafa. In fact the most important thing for horses and ponies is that the hay is as clean and free from dust and mould spores as possible. The nutritional value of any hay deteriorates after twelve months.

Silage can be fed to horses, as big bales, although it is vital that the plastic wrapping has not been damaged; if it has, the silage may have developed harmful bacteria. This is bought off the farm. Note that clamp silage as fed to dairy cows contains bacteria which are potentially fatal to all equines, so never allow a horse or pony access to such silage. HorseHage is a vacuum-packed semi-wilted forage available on the open market; it is quite high in protein so may not be suitable for smaller, fatter ponies, and horses may be fed a correspondingly reduced concentrate ration.

PROBLEM Forage – grass, hay and bagged silage – is the basis of a horse's diet, and essential for the proper functioning of his gut. What are the different types of forage available, and what sort should the average owner chose?

Choosing compound feeds

PROBLEM   What are compound feeds, and how does an owner know which one to choose for the individual horse?

Below: baled dried grass; coarse mix; complete cubes

SOLUTION   Compound feeds (formula feeds in the USA) are those that comprise ingredients that have been selected to provide a totally balanced diet for the horse. Each separate ingredient will have been analysed in the laboratory and will only have been added in such quantities that the total feed contains all of a horse's daily nutritional requirements. Compound feeds come in three distinct forms:

- complete feeds, which contain both the forage and concentrate portion of a horse's diet;
- concentrate cubes and mixes, a complete balanced ration of 'hard' feed that is fed in conjunction with forage such as hay or grass;
- cereal balancers, which are fed with other ingredients to 'balance' the feed.

There are three main advantages of compound feeds for the horse owner:
- they are convenient;
- they ensure the horse is receiving a balanced diet;
- they are used up quickly, which means all vitamins and minerals stay viable.

Feeding horses is far from straightforward as every single one has a slightly different temperament, metabolism, workload and so on. Equine nutritionists have made a lifetime study of feeding horses and all this specialist knowledge goes into formulating these products. It therefore makes sense for the individual horse owner to take advantage of this knowledge, and not to think that he can do better by mixing his own straight feeds such as oats, barley and maize: he should stick to a well recognised manufacturer who clearly labels each foodstuff. Guidelines should be given on the suitability of the feed for a given purpose, and the average quantities that should be fed. For example, if an owner has a 15.2hh middleweight horse weighing about 1,000lb (450kg) who competes in riding club activities most weekends, the bag of feed should clearly direct them to the quantities that should be fed. Most major manufacturers have a range of products to suit all levels of work and types of horse, ranging from racehorse cubes and mixes to quiet or paddock mixes, and branching out in specialist fields such as breeding mixes and rearing diets; therefore with a little experimentation every owner should be able to find a diet that suits his horse.

Hidden extras

SOLUTION Such an attitude is understandable, if not totally logical. As humans we would not eat anything unless we could see what it was, and this attitude is carried over into the feeding of horses. If left to his own devices, however, the horse would select foods with his sense of smell and taste rather than by sight. While a bag of feed should have all the ingredients listed, many owners are sceptical that there are lots of hidden extras only put in to 'bulk up' the feed. Generally this is simply not the case, however, especially with recognised manufacturers, and particularly as *by law* they now need to list what is in their products.

Owners should also bear in mind that while they can recognise straight feeds such as oats or barley, they have no way of determining their nutritional quality. Obviously they will be able to judge whether they are mouldy or dry, or clean or dusty, but they have no way of determining their nutrients. A bag of compound feed will provide this information however, and will list the protein, energy, fat and mineral levels for example, so very little is left to chance. An owner who insists on feeding straights leaves quite a lot to chance because a single straight such as oats can have protein levels ranging from 6 to 16 per cent alone – think of the difference this would make to the horse's feed. This is an example of only one straight, so owners should consider the implications if four or five straights were making up the horse's ration.

PROBLEM One of the reasons some owners do not like to feed compound feeds is because they cannot see what is in them. Is this attitude a sensible one, and if not, why not?

Extruded or micronised?

SOLUTION Extruded and micronised feeds are those that have been processed to make them easily digested by the horse. Traditionally, owners would have cooked barley – 'boiled barley' – in order to achieve the same result. The 'cooking' (extrusion or micronising) process is carried out in order to 'pre-digest' the cereal starch; this enables breakdown and absorption of the starch by the horse's digestive system to take place far more efficiently and quickly.

Such feeds have high levels of digestible energy, which means smaller quantities can be fed in order to achieve the same energy levels as higher quantities of non-processed feeds. This is of benefit to competition horses who need the energy but not a full tummy; and to the fussy feeder who requires the nutrition but will not consume very much feed.

PROBLEM What are extruded and micronised feeds, and of what benefit are they to the horse?

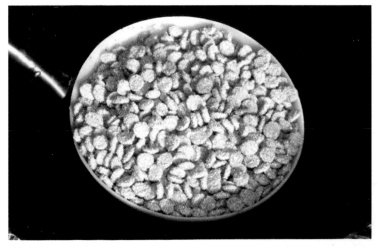

Extruded barley with linseed

Are supplements really necessary?

PROBLEM   Owners are often put under tremendous commercial pressure to buy supplements for their horses because advertising and literature suggests that such supplements will make their horse perform well, or feel better. Clever advertising can often make owners feel that unless they are feeding supplements they are not doing their best for their horse. Do such supplements do what they claim, or is it really a lot of hype?

SOLUTION   The benefit of adding supplements to a horse's feed depends entirely on the way the horse is kept, his diet and whether or not he is actually deficient in any nutrients. A supplement may be defined as an addition to a horse's diet designed to complete the ration – that is, to make up for a deficiency. Thus feeding supplements to a horse who has no deficiencies is pointless, and may even be harmful. However, even though a pasture may appear to be ideal, it can be deficient in terms of essential nutrients. Many paddocks are new leys rather than permanent pastures, and do not contain the variety of herbage that permanent ones do; moreover they are also often over-grazed and poorly managed, resulting in various deficiencies. If compound feeds are given to the horse in the quantities as directed by the manufacturers, then supplements should be unnecessary. However, the two problems are first, that many horse owners do not follow manufacturers' guidelines, preferring to offer their horse a 'bit of this and a bit of that'; and second, that manufacturers usually put in a lot of micro-nutrients that are cheap such as vitamin A and D or trace minerals such as copper, but fail to include sufficient levels of the more expensive ones.

Furthermore a horse eats for the sake of eating, rather that being selective because he needs the ingredients. In conclusion, unless the horse can eat a diverse range of flora, or be provided with a totally balanced ration that is matched to his particular needs, then the addition of supplements *is* beneficial.

DOES YOUR HORSE REALLY NEED SUPPLEMENTS?

The owner is left with the question of which supplements to choose, as there are hundreds on the market. Often it is felt that a broad-spectrum supplement will cover all eventualities, but usually this is not the case, and the horse will need more than one supplement. For example, normal vitamin/mineral supplements are often inadequate in terms of meeting the calcium and sodium requirements of working horses fed on cereal diets, and they often fail to meet the requirement of the horse for vitamin E as well. Such horses may therefore require electrolytes, a source of calcium, a broad-spectrum supplement and possibly a specialist supplement as well. Where the demands on a horse are high, it is often a good idea to involve an equine nutritionist who will be able to analyse the requirements of the horse and establish suitable supplementation where required.

Probiotics

PROBLEM Probiotics are said to be very beneficial to horses in times of illness or stress. What are probiotics, and what role do they play in the horse's digestive system?

SOLUTION Probiotics are naturally occurring micro-organisms that help to restore the natural balance of healthy micro-organisms in the horse's gut. They are the opposite of antibiotics which can strip the gut of their essential micro-organisms. It is therefore beneficial to use probiotics after a course of antibiotic, or during times of stress or feed change when the gut's micro-organisms can be greatly affected. In the latter circumstance the horse may succumb to conditions such as diarrhoea, and he may not be digesting his feed properly. A course of probiotics is an efficient way of introducing healthy micro-organisms back into the gut that begin to work straightaway and therefore re-establish healthy digestion. They are available in feed, supplement or paste form.

Yeast compounds and preparations containing Yeasacc work in a different way but with the same aim – to improve feed digestion. Yeasacc is definitely of benefit to 'poor doers'.

Salt

PROBLEM It is well documented that salt is bad for humans and that we must try to cut down on salt intake. Is this the same for horses?

SOLUTION Equine diets tend to be low in salt, and yet a horse's sweat contains a high level of sodium. In general therefore, the horse does need salt supplementation. Providing a horse with a salt lick will help, but as horses are not nutritionally wise, they will not always take in the amount of salt their body needs. Horses who sweat a great deal – endurance horses or eventers for example – should have salt added to their feed in quantities of about a teaspoon three times daily. Electrolytes given directly after exercise will also be beneficial for such horses.

Electrolytes

PROBLEM It is well known that hard-working horses may require electrolytes after demanding work where they have been sweating a great deal. What are electrolytes, and what are their benefits?

SOLUTION Electrolytes (now more commonly referred to as body salts) are mineral salts contained in the blood plasma of the horse. When a horse sweats he can lose considerable levels of sodium, calcium, potassium, phosphorus, magnesium and chlorine – collectively referred to as blood salts, or electrolytes. Providing electrolytes therefore ensures that the horse's fluid levels are maintained after exertion, and this helps to prevent dehydration.

Loss of blood salts and dehydration is not confined to the top competition horse. Unfit horses working in hot weather can also succumb to the effects of dehydration, and because sweat evaporates so quickly during heat the owner may not even be aware of it.

Horses cannot store electrolytes, so feeding them before an event is pointless. If an owner suspects his horse has sweated considerably – and owners should remember that this may not be obvious – then offering electrolytes soon after work, and for up to a day after hard work, can help redress the effects of dehydration.

Electrolytes are available in powder, paste or liquid form and can

be fed in the feed or put into water in line with the manufacturers' instructions. Where a horse is felt to be dehydrated, he should be given the paste form so than an owner is certain they have been taken in as quickly as possible. Many horses do not like electrolytes in water so plain water should be offered as well.

To check if a horse is dehydrated and so will require electrolytes, an owner should perform either the pinch test, or the capillary refill test. The pinch test involves pinching a layer of skin between the fingers to see how quickly it springs back into place. If it returns almost immediately the horse is probably not dehydrated, but if it takes time to spring back so that it stays ridged without being held, then he probably is.

The capillary refill test involves depressing the horse's gums with the thumb. When the thumb is removed, the area underneath will be white, and the longer the gum takes to return to its normal pink state, the more dehydrated the horse. However, the capillary refill test needs an educated eye for an accurate assessment.

The capillary refill test can be used by an experienced person to help determine the level of dehydration

The 'pinch test' is an easy way of assessing whether or not a horse is dehydrated

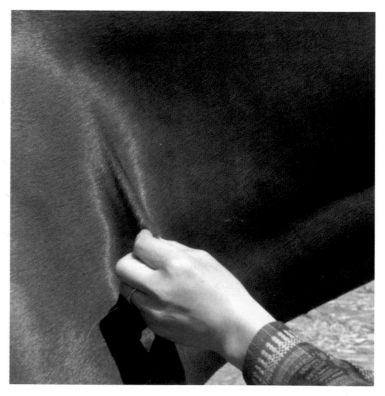

A bit fishy

PROBLEM Is cod liver oil a good additive for horses?

SOLUTION Cod liver oil is one of the most common types of supplement available to horse owners. Many owners feel that if it is good for them, then it must be good for their horse; however this is not always the case. First, although it does go through a deodorising process, cod liver oil still *smells* fishy, and it can put more fussy feeders off their food. Second, it has a high content of the fat-soluble vitamins A and D; these vitamins are stored in the fat deposits and liver of the horse, so reserves can be built up. Thus a horse grazing during the spring and summer months will build up his reserves of these vitamins, so it is in fact easy for an owner to 'overdose' his horse if he adds more in the way of cod liver oil, particularly if a compound feed containing these vitamins is also being fed.

The horse is able to make vitamin D in the skin, but he needs sunlight on his back in order to do so. Therefore a horse grazing out during the summer months is highly unlikely to be deficient. However, where a horse is stabled, has limited access to grass, or is rugged when at grass, his levels of vitamin D may be low. Vitamin D is required for the efficient absorption of calcium and phosphorous which helps to keep bones strong. Where vitamin D is thought to be in short supply the addition of cod liver oil will be beneficial, but an owner should check to see what levels are included in any compound feeds as well.

The horse requires sun on his back in order to produce vitamin D within the body

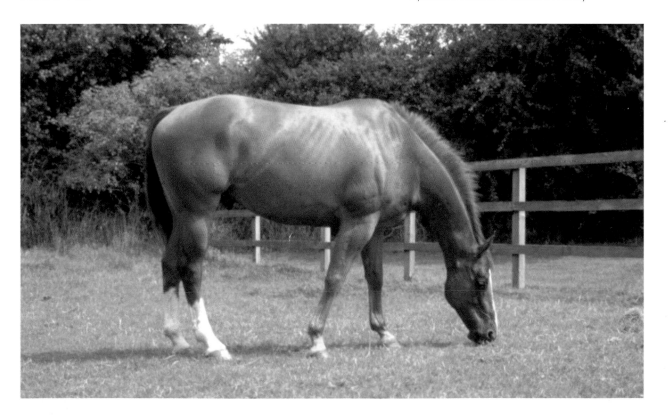

Herbs as balancers

SOLUTION Herbs are certainly beneficial, both for deficiencies and for performance. They contain a wide variety of balanced nutrients and chemicals, which can be beneficial when the horse's demand for nutrients rises as his system's demands increase. However, they should not be fed to such an extent that an imbalance occurs: once the horse's system is receiving all the nutrients it requires, an excess of herbs will simply upset the system, not improve it. The greatest use of herbs in the nutritional sense is when a horse is known to be deficient of something; following a correct diagnosis, the horse owner then has the opportunity of choosing a natural supplement from a biological plant source to balance the horse's system. Thus feeding herbs takes a little common sense, patience and a degree of observation and monitoring.

Another benefit of feeding herbs is that they do not contravene any of the rules set by the governing bodies of certain disciplines. This is especially useful for performance horses, because with the aid of herbs they can often cope with a strenuous workload without suffering ill effects. The effect of herbs is a cumulative one, and it takes time for them to act on the horse's system before the full benefits can be appreciated. Proprietary brands will give an indication of how much to add to the horse's feed, but as always, each horse is an individual and may need more or less than the stated amount.

PROBLEM Why do many owners feed herbs? Do they really have medicinal and nutritional benefits, or are they simply another fad that is at present in fashion?

(Opposite) As well as feeding one or two particular herbs, the owner also has the choice of feeding a herbal mix devised for a specific purpose, such as calming a horse down

Garlic

SOLUTION Garlic is probably one of the most widely used feed supplements, and its uses and actions are many and varied. First, it has a history of use in respiratory disorders, and horses suffering from allergies, coughs and colds will find relief from its expectorant and stimulant properties. Additionally it has been found beneficial:
- for horses prone to laminitis;
- as a fly repellent;
- in the control of sweet itch;
- for fighting infection as an antibiotic;
- as a blood cleanser;
- in the reduction of worms;
- in cases of arthritis and rheumatism;
- in reducing blood cholesterol and blood pressure.

Its essential oils contain vitamins A, B2, B3 and C, sulphur, crotonaldehyde, minerals and trace elements. It is usually purchased as a convenient powder which is measured into the feed, but it can also be supplied as a syrup, or fresh, or as oil capsules. Pulped garlic can be valuable when applied externally as a poultice on infected wounds as it has antiseptic and anti-inflammatory powers.

PROBLEM Garlic is an extremely popular feed additive. What does it do for the horse, and how is it fed?

Garlic in whole, powdered and pulp form

Food for thought

PROBLEM
Feeding bran is said to be bad for horses. Is this true, and if so, why?

SOLUTION
The purpose of feeding bran is to add fibre to a horse's diet. However, bran is low in both calcium and protein so it can cause deficiencies in the diet. As it also has a laxative effect, it is of little use in horse diets. A far better way of adding fibre to a horse's diet is by mixing chaff with the feed. Chaffs most usually consist of either pure hay, alfalfa, hay and straw, or alfalfa and straw. In order to make chaff more appetising to horses and to bind it all together, molasses is often added.

Ratios of rations

PROBLEM
Calcium and phosphorus levels cause great concern to owners, especially those of young horses on diets mixed from 'straights'. What can an owner do to ensure the ratios of these macro minerals are correct, and what are the consequences of an imbalance?

SOLUTION
Calcium and phosphorus are minerals required in fairly large quantities by the horse, and they are of special concern in youngstock because they are essential for normal bone growth, development and maintenance. The body's ratio of calcium:phosphorus is 1.7:1, and the owner should aim to reflect this ratio in the feeding regime he instigates for his horse, or at least to achieve a minimum of 1.5:1. Many traditional foodstuffs provide an unbalanced ratio intake, for instance:

- Oats can have a calcium:phosphorus ratio of approximately 1:5;
- Wheat bran can have a calcium:phosphorus ratio of approximately 1:8;
- Sugar beet can have a calcium:phosphorus ratio of approximately 1:1

It is easy to see, therefore, that a diet which includes high levels of oats or bran can lead to an unbalanced intake of calcium and phosphorus. An imbalance or deficiency of calcium in the diet has been implicated in DOD (developmental orthopaedic disease) and is thought to be a contributing factor to the onset of azoturia (see also page 113). An imbalance or deficiency of phosphorus in the diet has been implicated in bone abnormalities and retarded growth in young horses. It therefore becomes clear that feeding horses is an art, and unless owners are aware of the levels of minerals and suchlike that straights contain, they would be safer sticking to a proprietary brand of compound feed (see page 138). Most compound feeds work to a calcium:phosphorus level of 2:1 which when fed at recommended levels will meet the daily requirement of horses.

Every sack of feed should contain a nutritional breakdown of its contents

Best foot forward

CAUSE Poor horn quality is an extremely common problem and is often linked to deficiencies in nutrition, so yes, nutrition does play a part.

SOLUTION First, it helps to feed a horse with poor hooves dried, chopped lucerne, as it has higher levels of vitamin A, protein and calcium, all of which are necessary for healthy hoof growth, than other types of chaff or hay products. And yes, there are numerous additives on the market that claim to improve the quality of horn growth; however, their effectiveness depends on the horse's existing diet, his hoof condition and hoof conformation. An owner should realise that no product is going to correct hooves which are faulty due to conformation or neglect.

Providing the hooves have been attended to regularly and correctly by a good farrier, adding pure seaweed powder to the feed is beneficial.

PROBLEM Does nutrition have a role to play in the quality of a horse's hooves? Also, are there any particular feed additives that might encourage healthy growth and prevent hooves from cracking?

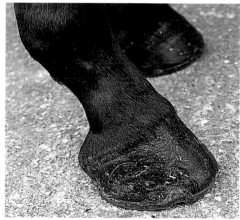

A 'dumped' hoof. The condition has been caused by incorrect farriery

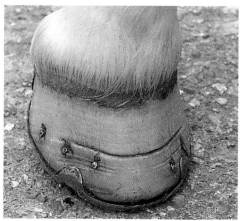

A hoof which clearly shows the classic rings associated with poor nutrition

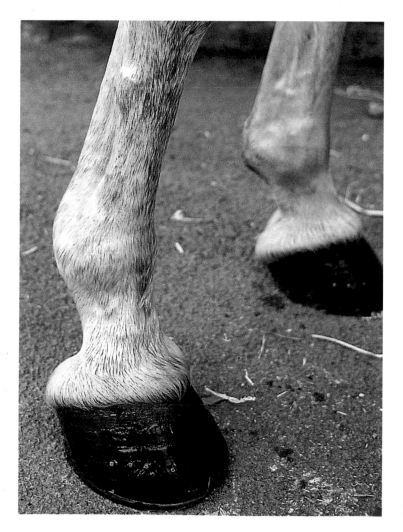

Left: Good, strong hooves

Sweet tooth

PROBLEM How long a shelf-life does sugar beet have, what forms does it come in, and for how long does it need to be soaked before feeding?

SOLUTION The storage conditions for sugar beet must be dry, cool and airtight, and are important because it will readily become mouldy in damp conditions. In ideal conditions molassed sugar-beet pulp or cubes can be stored for up to a year without detriment; for the average owner who may not have ideal conditions in their feed room, however, a period of no longer than three months is advised.

Both forms of sugar beet – shredded pulp or pelleted – readily absorb moisture, so it is absolutely *essential* that sugar beet is soaked before feeding to horses. Water should be added in quantities that will allow the pulp or pellets to swell up to their maximum size: for pulp this is usually twice the volume of water to pulp, and for pellets, four times the volume of water to pellets, but manufacturer's guidelines should always be carefully followed. If a horse were to eat unsoaked sugar-beet pulp or pellets the consequences could be fatal.

Sugar beet pellets will take longer to hydrate than sugar-beet pulp: ten or twelve hours for pulp is normal, while pellets may need up to twenty-four hours. After twenty-four hours, however, especially in hot weather, the sugar beet may start to ferment, so it should be used up quickly otherwise digestive complaints may occur.

Sugar beet cubes (above) and sugar beet pulp (below): never feed unsoaked sugar beet cubes to horses

SWEET TIP

To prevent it freezing, the sugar beet can be soaked in an insulated box – the type of cool-box that may be used on a picnic. If one of these cannot be obtained for this purpose, putting the sugar beet tub inside a dustbin partly filled with straw will also stop it from freezing over, providing the dustbin lid is put on!

Food hygiene

SOLUTION As soon as feeds are delivered they should be stored in a clean, dry, well ventilated barn or room. Food for immediate use can be put into clean, vermin-proof feed bins – such as purpose-made galvanised ones, or clean dustbins – while bags to be stored can be put onto pallets, covered with a blanket and stored at least 3in (7.6cm) from any wall. To prevent the risk of contamination, an owner should ensure that feed-bin lids are always put back directly after the feeds are mixed.

Hay straight from the field is still full of moisture and should be stored with airways between stacks in a ventilated barn for about six months before use. It should not be stored in a garage or closed shed, as this will encourage condensation and thus mould will develop.

Food hygiene continues when preparing feeds. Separate utensils should be used for both dry and wet feeds, and these should be cleaned after use, including any knives used for slicing carrots and apples. If feeds are to be dampened with water or sugar beet, this should not be added until immediately prior to feeding.

Once a horse has eaten his feed, the manger should be removed for cleaning, dried, and then replaced to prevent injuries from occurring should a horse get caught on the manger holder. Once a feed manger becomes split or cracked it should be replaced as it will soon begin to harbour bacteria no matter how efficient the cleaning routine.

Finally, it is useless to ensure such high levels of hygiene if watering facilities are neglected. Automatic waterers need turning off and scrubbing out daily, as do water buckets, and field troughs should be cleaned once a week.

PROBLEM Once food has been collected from the mill or delivered from a feed merchant, how should it be stored to ensure it stays in top condition for feeding?

Storing feedstuffs in clean, dry and organised conditions will save you both time and money through avoiding unnecessary wastage

New hay

PROBLEM How soon can new season hay be fed after harvesting and is there anything an owner should do to help his horse become accustomed to the change from one season's hay to another?

SOLUTION New hay has quite a high protein content compared to older hay, especially if the hay was made early in the season. This high protein content can make it quite rich for horses, causing digestive upsets and even colic if fed too soon. Hay therefore benefits from being allowed to mature before feeding, and a period of between three to six months is recommended, depending on ventilation and storage. The rule of introducing new feeds gradually should also be observed, so while there are still supplies of old hay, the owner should mix in a small quantity of the new. Over a period of weeks this can be built up until the old hay has gone and the new hay has totally replaced it; this gives a horse's gut micro-organisms (see page 141) time to adjust to the new foodstuff, and can help to stretch out a dwindling supply of old hay.

Feeding yearlings

PROBLEM There is often a lot of conflicting advice given about feeding yearlings. How can an owner ensure his yearling is being fed correctly, and what are the dangers of an incorrect diet at this age?

SOLUTION During the summer months, if grazing is good, a yearling should not require supplementary feeding. He should be able to live out day and night quite happily, and while he should be checked daily, he will benefit from being left to mature mentally and physically. If grazing is poor, however, then supplementary feeding will be necessary, and an owner cannot do better than to feed a reputable brand of yearling cubes or coarse mix that has been specifically formulated with the needs of the youngster's growth in mind. It is a mistake for the owner to try and balance his own feeds when this has already been expertly and scientifically done. Using a single brand of nuts or mix also ensures that each bag is fresh when used, which means there will be no loss of vitamins or minerals. Generally, 2lb (900g) of yearling cubes, 2lb of high quality chaff and ad-lib hay will be quite sufficient to see a yearling through to his second year. While owners may have friends who mean to offer good advice, they would be better reading a few really good books on the subject such as *Feeding Horses and Ponies* by Susan McBane (David & Charles) and *Equine Nutrition* by Derek Cuddiford (The Crowood Press).

Feeding fatties

SOLUTION   The obvious answer is that such ponies need to be put on to grazing that is sparse, or of low nutritional quality. However, actually to put such a solution into practice can be very difficult, because every horse owner does all he can to create lush, high quality pastures; so finding the complete opposite can prove a problem! Starving a pony by putting him in a stable without food is not the answer, but with the advent of safe electric fencing it is quite easy to section off a corner of the field that will have little or no grass once the pony has initially eaten it down. Supplementary feeding in the form of hay will be necessary to ensure proper gut function, but in time, a level of feeding can be established that keeps the pony slim enough. Alternatively, a strip-grazing system can be employed where the electric fencing is moved along as the pony eats all the available grass in a strip at a time.

PROBLEM   Many owners have great difficulty in keeping small native ponies in lean condition. Often they seem to live on thin air, receiving nothing but grass. How can such ponies be slimmed down?

Where strip-grazing cannot be employed, a pony can have a muzzle fitted to prevent him gorging himself. Such a muzzle should be made of leather and have about eight or ten holes cut into the bottom so that small amounts of grass can be consumed. This solution has the benefit of mimicking the pony's natural lifestyle because he will have to roam about quite a lot in order to find grass long enough to poke through the holes, and will therefore have to work far harder for less feed. Psychologically and nutritionally this is a much better system than leaving the pony without food for long periods

Older horses

PROBLEM Older horses can prove more difficult to keep weight on than their younger companions. Are there any special diets for older horses, or can an owner create his own special diet to suit his old horse's needs?

SOLUTION Before any thought is given to feeding regimes for the older horse, the owner should first have his horse's teeth checked. Older horses can suffer a great deal from worn or damaged teeth – in the wild it is the condition of the horse's teeth which governs his life-span – and if they are left untreated this can lead to great pain and a deterioration in condition. Sometimes the teeth are so worn that there is little that can be done; even so, such a horse may still be able to put on condition if his owner takes the time to concoct a highly nutritious diet that can be made into a gruel that the horse slurps up. This may sound a little absurd, but such measures have improved the quality of life for many an old horse.

Providing the teeth are fine, the owner should next ensure that the horse does not have a high worm burden.

Only when these two factors have been established should changes of diet be considered.

The most common cause of an older horse losing condition is simply because his digestive system is not working as efficiently as it used to. In order to counteract this, an older horse should be provided with higher levels of digestible protein, easily offered in the form of extruded or micronised feeds (see page 139). However, some of these feeds are quite hard and crunchy, so the older horse may appreciate them being soaked a little in warm water first to soften them. An older horse's protein requirement can rise to around 14 per cent in order to counteract heat loss and to maintain condition (note, too, that his heating mechanisms may also be failing, so rugging up may prove essential). There are now special mixes for older horses, and in general these are far better than anything owners can hope to mix themselves. One should be chosen that satisfies the need for extra-digestible protein and higher levels of vitamins and minerals. Many feed companies now have helplines and it is a good idea to give these a call to talk to a nutritionist direct about any specific problems.

A gruel can be made by soaking extruded feeds in warm water before feeding

---

TIP

Older horses may benefit from the addition of probiotics or Yeasacc in the feed (see page 141). By ensuring that his gut micro-organisms are at their optimum the older horse will be able to make the very best use of the feed he is able to consume.

Bolting feed

SOLUTION   There are three main consequences of a horse bolting his feed:

- choke;
- colic;
- lack of nourishment..

Choke is a recognised health complication that may require veterinary treatment (see also page 100); colic can occur as a result of the horse being unable to digest unchewed food; and a lack of nourishment can occur because the food passes through the system whole (undigested).

To slow a horse down, 'padding' such as chaff, sugar beet and succulents can be added to the feed; these encourage the horse to slow down and chew more carefully because they are not so easily taken up and swallowed whole without first being chewed. If this method fails, the horse can be physically prevented from gulping into his feed by putting things in the manger which he will have to eat round; for example, house bricks, salt licks and *large* round stones can all be used to good effect.

Sometimes changing the type of manger works, such as using one the horse has to put his head into, or a shallow one. Horses tend to dislike putting their head into a container over which they cannot see, so they will take a mouthful and then withdraw their head in order to observe what is going on around them, rather than keeping their head down in the container and gobbling through their feed. Conversely, some horses feel less threatened if fed in a shallow bowl and so will become more relaxed and calmer when feeding. As with most aspects of horse management, knowing the individual horse is important, and finding the right feeding environment can be just as important to a horse who bolts his feed as finding the right type of feed for a fussy eater.

PROBLEM   Horses who bolt their food can be just as much a worry to their owners as those who will not eat at all. How can a horse be encouraged to eat his feed more slowly, and what are the consequences of him bolting his feed?

TIP

Where a horse bolts his hay, an owner can try putting one haynet inside another to slow him down, or use a haynet with smaller holes so that he has to work harder for his hay.

Getting the type of feed container right for the horse can often be the key to unlocking his feeding anxieties; buckets are not suitable as they can easily tip over

Palatability

PROBLEM Is the palatability of food important to a horse, or are most horses satisfied with whatever food they are given?

SOLUTION While many horses will eat the same food day in, day out, it does help to keep a horse interested in his food by making it inviting for him. When considering this, an owner should take into account the texture and variety of the feed, and also the horse's senses of taste and smell, because these are highly developed and the horse will soon discard something that tastes or smells unpleasant to him. This can cause a problem if introducing new foodstuffs to a horse that smell and taste odd to him. Therefore anything new in the diet should be added gradually until he gets accustomed to it and accepts it.

Conversely, tastes the horse likes can be used to disguise unwelcome things in the feed such as wormers. Liquid molasses or sugar beet can be used to cloak such odd smells and tastes, and sometimes the horse can be duped in this way into eating something that he would usually reject.

It is thought that a horse appreciates different textures in his feed. While a horse grazing lush spring grass seems quite happy eating an identical meal every day, a horse stabled for most of the time will appreciate a variety of textures. This does not mean the ingredients of the diet are changed every day, simply that each meal has an assortment of textures, shapes and tastes, such as is contained in a coarse mix. Adding succulents such as carrots and apples will also add to the palatability of the meal.

Fussy feeders

PROBLEM What can be done to encourage a fussy feeder to eat, and are there any recognised practices that tend to create fussy feeders that can be avoided?

SOLUTION Fussy feeders can usually be put into one of three categories:
- those who turn up their noses at many different types of feed;
- those who are easily distracted from eating;
- those who fail to empty their feed bowls.

While fussy feeders may have extra-sensitive palates, they are usually types who suffer from anxiety and psychological problems. Where the horse is thought to have a sensitive palate the owner must simply go through a process of elimination until a foodstuff is found that the horse likes. The addition of succulents to the diet may help, but essentially an acceptable feed must be found that provides a fully balanced diet.

The anxious horse should be fed in a peaceful and quiet place where there are no sudden noises or hubbub or constant interruptions. There should certainly be no threat from any other horse, and the horse in question should be allowed plenty of time in which to eat his food. Also, the feed should be divided into three or four small ones if possible, as fussy feeders will often eat little feeds offered frequently whereas they will never clean up a large feed (also see Palatability above as the same guidelines apply to fussy feeders).

An anxious horse will often hop from his feed bin back to the door in order not to miss anything that is going on around him

Index

ER